Hope you enjoy!
Nov 1st 2019.

MIAMI BOUND

'Miami'
by
Joan

MIAMI BOUND

John Boam

Miami Bound

This book is a memoir and as such reflects the author's impression of events as told by those who experienced them.

Production 2017

For updates about Miami Bound along with more photos and videos please visit his website www.miamibound.co.uk or Facebook Miami Bound Showjumping Pony (@MiamiBoundshowjumper)

Cover photo of Miami Bound. In the background is the field on the Boam's farm where he was born in south west Scotland.

ISBN 978-1-9997162-0-2

Printed and bound in Great Britain by Bell and Bain Ltd, Glasgow

Dedication

While there have been many remarkable showjumping ponies over the years, it takes a special quality for one to perform at their best for multiple young riders season after season. These super ponies are experienced specialists; trusted, clever and reliable.

This book is dedicated to those small equines, who make dreams come true. Among other things, they teach us the valuable principle that success does not come without hard work and determination.

CONTENTS

PREFACE

There have been lots of books written about famous horses, but very few about ponies.

This book started out as a family keepsake about a pony we bred on our sheep farm in Scotland who went on to become a showjumping champion. Throughout his twenty-year career in showjumping he won most of the biggest prizes in Europe, before retiring back to the farm where he was born.

As we interviewed his past riders, it soon became clear that there ought to be a book written about this very special pony and his adventures. This story isn't just about a pony and his achievements, it's about the bonds and the memories of all his young riders and how he has helped shape their future careers.

All career horsemen and women have had a special pony in their lives. Miami Bound has had fourteen competitive riders and all have a special memory of him. This book has turned into a heart-warming story of Miami Bound's life: tales of aspirations, courage, hard work, determination, disappointments and accomplishments through his twenty-year career.

As a family we are so thankful to be able to retire

Miami Bound at home on our farm, made even more special since we still have his mother, Gypsy.

So this book is a celebration of the life of 'MB', may he have a long and fulfilling retirement.

John Boam

Breeder John Boam and the now retired Miami Bound, giving him one of his favourite treats, a polo mint!

Miami Bound Jumping 1.45m at the Horse of the Year Show with Thomas Whitaker as they won the Leading Junior Showjumper of the Year final in 2006. Image by Anthony Reynolds LMPA

INTRODUCTION

Miami Bound is a handsome grey gelding who rose from humble beginnings to become a champion showjumping pony. He stands just a fraction over 14.1hh (145cm) and was born on a stormy morning in June 1991 out of a coloured Welsh pony called Gypsy.

There are few ponies who have achieved the heights of fame that this remarkable pony has. He had fourteen competitive riders and formed a special partnership with each one. During his competitive career he won major National Championships in the UK, Ireland and Norway, as well as pony Grands Prix's all around Europe. He also won puissance, six bar and two fence challenge competitions and was a member of the winning pony Nations Cup teams for both Ireland and Great Britain.

Miami Bound has a short stride, which made his job a lot harder. The fences in top pony competitions are often bigger than those jumped by most horses at around 1.30m to 1.45m high! The jumps are so wide you could easily stand with arms outstretched and still not touch the front and back poles. Most of the successful 148cm jumping ponies are like mini horses, with long strides, which makes it easier for them to jump the big combinations.

This is where Miami Bound surprised the experts. His quick-thinking ingenuity to calculate the right stride, along with his superb jumping ability, has made him one of the most successful jumping ponies of his time.

Miami Bound was always a crowd pleaser in the jump off and could often pull off unimaginable turns to win a class, much to the delight of the audience. His determination seemed to show though, as he would put his ears back and swish his tail, sometimes kicking back after crossing the finish line as if to say 'catch me if you can!'

Some of his outstanding achievements include qualifying and competing at Horse of the Year Show (HOYS) in an impressive seven National Championships, with five different riders. He was champion there three times and runner up one year. To qualify for this prestigious show – which is the biggest pony competition in Europe, if not the world – is a huge achievement and only the very best have a chance of winning.

Miami Bound won the Blue Chip Junior Newcomers final at HOYS in 2000 with Lauley Squibb and was eighth in the Squibb and Davis Junior Foxhunter final that year. This combination also won the Squibb Group Junior Foxhunter Masters at the Festival of Showjumping and were presented their prize by Lauley's mother and class sponsor, Pat Squibb.

The following year he was second in the Leading Junior Showjumper of the Year final with Ellen Whitaker at HOYS. The jumps are up to 1.45m high with triple bars up to 1.65m wide. Ellen and Miami Bound also won the 148cm Grand Prix at both the Scope Festival of

Showjumping and South View Equestrian Centre. Ellen's younger brother, Joe, rode him briefly at the end of that season, before he was sold to Ireland.

Kathryn Fitzgibbon had picked out the grey gelding for her daughter, Nicola, and the pair went on to win every major pony competition in Ireland together.

They were Irish National Champions two years in a row and Speed Champions simultaneously one year. They also won the prestigious 148cm Dublin Horse Show Championship, the Grand Prix in Diest, Belgium, the Grand Prix in Fontainebleau, France and were part of the winning Irish Nations Cup pony team in CSIOP Freudenberg Germany in 2003.

In the prime of his career Miami Bound rarely touched a pole or refused. He always rose to a big occasion and had a tremendous jump. He would jump from almost any position and was very fast against the clock.

In one puissance competition with Nicola he cleared a 1.75m wall with ease and much to the delight of the crowd they bravely attempted another go at a massive 1.85m wall. He nearly cleared that but his stifle gently nudged the top brick off. In another competition they won a six bar challenge, with six upright fences in a row and the last went up to 1.65m. They also won a two-fence challenge with two jumps in a row at 1.70m.

Miami Bound was then sold from Ireland to Italy where he spent just over two years with new rider Orsola Baggio and competed in various FEI (Federation Equestre Internationale) competitions around Europe.

In 2006 Steven Whitaker brought him back to the UK

for his son Thomas to compete. It was with Tom that Miami Bound won his first Leading Junior Showjumper of the Year title at HOYS, followed by a second win in 2007 with cousin George.

At the time of print he is only the second pony in history to have won the Leading Pony Showjumper of the Year title at HOYS for two consecutive years. The last pony to achieve this great feat was Kangaroo with Nicola Loffett in 1967.

Donald Whitaker, younger brother of Ellen, Joe and Tom, also had a successful season with Miami Bound in 2008. Together they won a big Grand Prix in Lummen, Belgium as well as qualifying for the Leading Pony Showjumper of the Year final at HOYS.

Jessica Crosby took over the ride in November 2008 when she was just 14 years old. They had eleven months together and in that time won ten open classes including wins at Scope's Festival of Showjumping and Wales and West's 148cm Open. Miami Bound again had good placings at major shows around the UK and Jessica gained valuable experience competing in some of the big pony European trials.

Miami Bound then spent five years in Norway. His first two years were with brother and sister Per and Lisa Ulven. Per and Lisa competed at all the major pony showjumping competitions including shows at Drammen in Norway, Odense in Denmark and Hengelo in the Netherlands. Per won a medal at the Norwegian championships with Miami Bound and won most of the classes they started. In the spring of 2012, Lisa competed on

Miami Bound in the Spanish Sunshine tour and they won nearly all the 1.10m and 1.20m classes together.

When Lisa outgrew Miami, he went on to teach young rider Nora Larsen Nalbant who was stabled on the same yard as the Ulven's. Miami Bound's final home in Norway was with aspiring rider Elin Martine Mehren, who was eleven years old when her trainer spotted the talented jumper for sale as a schoolmaster.

Breeder John's daughter, Katie, had kept in touch with his owners in Norway and they kindly sent pictures and updates. Katie recalls: "When I received an email asking if we would like to have him back to retire we were all overwhelmed and excited. It was wonderful to tell everyone especially Heather and Hugh who remained close friends. We all had kept cuttings from articles about his success and have pictures of him jumping framed on our walls."

In August 2015, Miami Bound came home to the farm where he was born, reunited with his mother, Gypsy. The rest of this book is about the life and character of this truly remarkable pony, who has had a lasting impression on his young riders and their families.

Miami Bound's experience in teaching younger riders in his later years has been so treasured and beautiful memories are shared in this book. As John says, 'We feel incredibly proud and grateful to share his amazing story'.

ACKNOWLEDGEMENTS

John Boam and family would like to express sincere thanks to the many people who have contributed to this book and all those who have played a part in Miami Bound's life and career.

Thanks to the help of Jacqueline Broderick of Lavender & White Publishing in helping the concept get started and to Charlotte Ricca-Smith for checking it over once finished.

It is heart-warming to know how loved and well cared for Miami Bound has been throughout his career. "We have been so surprised and thankful for all the enthusiasm from everyone who has shared their memories with us and thankful for his many talented young riders who gave him the opportunity to become a champion in the arena he loves" says John.

Special thanks to Heather Vance and her papa Hugh Patterson, Alan Fazakerley, Lauley and Claire Squibb as well as Les and Pat Squibb. Steven and Carole Whitaker, Ellen, Tom, Joe, Donald and George Whitaker as well as Jessica Crosby. We would also like to express our gratitude to the late Kathryn FitzGibbon for her role in recognising Miami Bound's talent and playing a key role in his success with daughter Nicola in Ireland. Special thanks to Nicola FitzGibbon and her father, Nick for their comments in this book. We are thankful for all of his riders and owners in Norway who looked after him so well; Per, Lisa and Lena Ulven, Nora Larsen Nalbant, Elin Martine Mehren and Ragnhild Eggum.

Appreciation for the professional photos of Miami Bound in competition to Anthony Reynolds LMPA, Tony Parkes Photographer, Steve Dawe at Real Time Imaging, Graham Loader Thefotographer, Suzanne Jones at Jumping Around and Maud Le Bel of Studforlife. Thanks to Dave Cameron photography and British Showjumping (BS) for the images taken for the BS magazine article in January 2017.

Last but not least a special thank you to our daughter Katie for the many hours researching and verifying records, typing and rewriting, and for looking after the ponies in their retirement.

We would still be interested to hear from anyone who can share more memories or photos with us so please do get in touch we'd love to hear from you.

Farming and Family Life

Miami Bound's breeder; John Boam and the family's love of horses

Miami Bound was bred in South West Scotland by the Boam family; farmers who were originally from the Peak District in Derbyshire.

John Boam was brought up on a small dairy farm in the Peak District. From an early age it was expected that the jobs on the farm came first and hobbies came second, if at all. One of the first tasks John learned was helping his mother feed the calves morning and night, before and after school.

His parents Molly and Frank had been brought up with working horses, they pulled the cart on the farm and would do a lot of the work tractors do these days. To have a horse or pony just for pleasure didn't come into their way of thinking.

It was a local retired army major who inspired John's love of riding. He rode a Dales cob and would call in at the farm to give John a ride up the lane. John soon started to pester his parents to buy him a pony, but to no avail, as they thought it was a passing fad. By the age of nine, and still pestering, his Gran took pity on him and bought him a donkey.

Far from the ideal first pony, the donkey would buck like a rodeo horse! John's father had to ride him first until he settled down enough for John to get on.

John thinks that donkey taught him to ride, as it bucked him off so many times he had to learn to sit tight. By the age of eleven his desire for a pony hadn't gone, and his parents finally relented. They bought him a newly broken three-year-old New Forest pony, which John did everything with – from Pony Club to pony racing and hunt to showjumping. The pony also rekindled his parents' interest and they helped John in his horsey quests.

Every autumn, a dealer would bring in ponies from Wales to the local market in Bakewell. John would always buy a couple of two-year-olds from him, which he would break and sell on the following year. His father encouraged him and it became John's little business within the farm. As John got bigger, so did the horses, which he has many interesting memories of. His mother Molly, in her later years and with more spare time, bred a few good Welsh ponies, too.

John's wife, Joan, also had a love of horses from an early age, but being one of a large family, owning a pony of her own was out of the question. As a young teenager, Joan and her school friend, Ann, would gladly accept a ride on any horse or pony on offer. They eventually found a farm which had horses they could ride, on the outskirts of Bolsover, their home village.

The horses belonged to Ian Adsetts who was a member of the British Showjumping Association (BSJA). He also broke and schooled ponies on the farm. Joan and Ann paid for a few riding lessons with Ian and then began to work for their rides instead. For a couple of years, all their free time was spent at the farm with the horses, riding and doing all kinds of jobs.

After leaving school, aged fifteen, Joan worked for Ian as a full-time groom, looking after the showjumping horses and helping re-train problem ponies. Ian would sometimes organise showjumping competitions on his farm and Joan and Ann would act as stewards.

At one of these shows they were a little annoyed at a young male rider as he knocked down most of the jumps in his classes. This meant they spent a lot of time running around, putting the poles back up again. Joan later found out the young man was none other than John Boam, her future husband. John explained later that his father, Frank, had ambitiously entered him into the big Open classes with his novice horse. Frank's attitude was if they were travelling a distance to a show they may as well enter every class!

When Joan was nineteen she eventually saved enough money to buy her own horse. Years later, after John and Joan were married and started farming on their own, all their horses had to be sold for the couple to buy their first dairy cows.

It was years later when their first daughter, Debbie, was five years old that a pony arrived on the farm again. Pixie was an 11.2hh Exmoor pony bought from a neighbour, an ideal first pony for Debbie.

Pixie had taught Debbie all the basic skills of horsemanship, as often happens with a first pony. Pixie was trusted, reliable and safe and she went on to teach Katie and Luke. The pony was such a part of the family that she often wandered into the farmhouse in Monyash, if the door was left open, as her paddock ran around the front and side of the house.

Needless to say, John and Joan's children had ponies from an early age. Their two daughters, Debbie and Katie, took to riding and loved ponies. However their two sons, James and Luke, loved a different kind of horsepower, preferring motorbikes to ponies.

Gypsy had come into their lives quite by chance. John had bought her while looking for something completely different. They had gone to see a local horse dealer intending to buy Silver, a 14.3hh ride and drive cob which they both could ride. John needed a horse to ride round the farm, to check the stock, while Joan wanted to ride out with Debbie on her hacks round the lanes.

Silver was a lovely grey cob, ideal for what they wanted and they agreed to buy him. As they were about to leave they noticed a pretty skewbald mare, about 13.2hh, in another stable. Enquiring about her, the dealer told them he had bought her three days earlier from Buith Wells Welsh pony horse sales. They asked if they could see her out of the stable, so the dealer put some tack on her and his nine-year-old daughter rode her around the arena and jumped a little cross pole. He then led them onto a busy main road next to his yard and Gypsy never flinched.

John and Joan's thoughts were the same: Gypsy seemed so sensible she would suit Debbie perfectly as her second pony. Debbie tried Gypsy in the arena and her big smile as she trotted and cantered around said it all. Gypsy was only three years old, but showed more maturity than ponies twice her age. The dealer asked five hundred pounds for her, which was a lot of money back then, especially without tack, but as a safe pony she was too good to miss. Debbie was thrilled!

Debbie and Gypsy soon became inseparable. They joined the High Peak Hunt branch of the Pony Club and enjoyed learning together. Gypsy proved to be a perfect second pony, and was willing, safe and great fun to ride. She also had tremendous jumping ability. The pair did everything together at Pony Club, but the one thing she excelled at was hunting.

Throughout the hunting season Debbie and Gypsy rode across the fields, some of which were used for the Flagg Point-to-Point races. Gypsy's ears pricked at the sound of the hunting horn and she was ready to go. She showed off her ability, keeping up with the bigger horses in the field, and often jumping better than them. Gypsy and Debbie flew over large dry stone walls, hedges and ditches. Both were brave and competitive and enjoyed the days out in the fresh Derbyshire air.

As their family had grown they soon realised the small dairy farm in Derbyshire could not support the family and a decision had to be made to look for a bigger farm. Land in Derbyshire was very expensive so John had to look further afield.

They eventually bought a beef and sheep farm in South West Scotland and although they didn't know anyone there, they agreed to try it for a year or so and see how things went. Now, 27 years later they are writing this book and two of their children – Katie and James – live on the same farm with their families.

The news that the family were relocating was difficult for fourteen-year-old Debbie who was devastated at the thought of moving to Scotland and missing the summer Pony Club camp with Gypsy and all her friends. Having to change schools and leave her friends behind was difficult, so a compromise was found. Debbie would move with the family to Scotland and return south for the summer, with Gypsy, to stay with her much-loved Grandma Molly in Monyash. Schools in Scotland finish for the summer before those in England, which allowed Debbie to attend the Pony Club camp.

After Debbie and Gypsy returned to the new farm in Scotland, and summer rolled into autumn, everyone adjusted to their new life. Debbie found it difficult being the new girl at school, but found comfort spending time with Gypsy.

The following spring Debbie was fast outgrowing Gypsy, so her parents bought her a new 15.2hh horse to compete in one day events, which was her favourite sport. A decision had to be made as to what to do with Gypsy. Debbie's sister, Katie, was only six years old and not yet ready to ride her yet. Although the thought of parting with Gypsy was very sad, it was decided to sell the mare, because she still had a lot to offer another young rider.

However, fate played her hand, as Gypsy proved hard to sell. Since Debbie had outgrown her, she had been turned out at grass and was just an ordinary 13.2hh skewbald pony, grazing with sheep. With no recent competition history and an unsightly fatty lump on the side of her neck, she didn't appeal to buyers.

Katie was growing rapidly and becoming a confident rider on Pepe, her Welsh Section A pony. When no buyer could be found for Gypsy, the decision was made to keep her for Katie to ride. In the meantime she would breed a foal.

John found a good local stallion for Gypsy. He was a small, grey Thoroughbred called Jay River, who lived on a farm at Glenluce near Stranraer. John agreed the £80 stud fee with his owner, Willard McGhee, and Gypsy was taken to the stud in the summer.

Willard's farm overlooked the vast sands of Luce Bay. Those sands had been used by local jockey Colin Adams who used the sands to train his race horses. It is interesting that the Galloway region has a strong connection to race-horse history and this ties in with Miami Bound's father, Jay River.

At the age of two Jay River won his first flat race and was in training with John Powney at Saville House in Newmarket. At three he won a sprint at Wolverhampton over a distance of five furlongs and the following year he got placed in his first run of the season. However, the diminutive colt didn't have a lot going for him as a race-horse, he hated wearing blinkers and didn't look much beside the other big sleek Thoroughbreds at Newmarket, but he was a trier. Although born brown he had turned grey by the time he was five.

With just a few wins in low-grade races, to most people

who came across him, Jay River was just a mediocre horse. A typical sort for running in seller races. With just a few wins in low grade races, as a stallion, he was suitable only for siring riding ponies or eventing types.

His stud fee was so reasonable few breeders ever looked into his bloodline. One of Jay River's ancestors was Bald Galloway, a famous stallion born in the 1700s. His bloodline can be found in some of the greatest horses the world has ever seen, including Shergar, Desert Orchid and the amazing showjumper Milton.

The origin of the name, Bald Galloway, is unsure. No one remembers whether it was because of his white face, or the local dialect pronouncing 'bald' instead of 'bold'.

What is known is that his great grandsire, Fenwick Barb, was said to have been the best of his time and his grandsire, Whynot, was even better. Bald Galloway went on to become Leading Sire in Great Britain and Ireland, a title awarded to the stallion whose offspring has won the most prize money during the flat racing season. It was for this reason he was such a popular choice for breeders in Britain, even at the high price of five guineas per mare.

His bloodline proliferated, spreading further and further, into war horses from Europe, the Americas and other far off lands. All his offspring had distinctive white faces and greys stood out amongst the bays, browns and blacks of the day.

In the autumn Gypsy returned home in foal to Jay River. Her tough, clever pony bloodlines mixing with those of the agile, fast, determined progeny of Bald Galloway.

Storm

Miami Bound's first name was Storm

As spring came around again Debbie would spend time rubbing Gypsy's ever expanding belly and talking to the unborn foal, telling it her secrets and hopes for the future. Debbie encouraged the foal to run faster, jump higher and escape the confines of the farm and explore the wide world that lay beyond Dumfries and Galloway.

These poignant moments they spent together helped Debbie focus and relieved the stress of studying for her exams. As the foal kicked inside Gypsy's belly Debbie felt the new life and it gave her hope for her own future. With her exams due to start in May, and the foal due in June, the times spent with Gypsy became Debbie's therapy.

At the top of the field where Gypsy grazed, the land opened into a flattish clearing surrounded by gorse. This spot has a panoramic view of the whole landscape, the house, the barns and yard. It was a great lookout for Gypsy who could see right to the woodland on the edge of the farm and all the way to the bay, where the sea glittered blue or a forbidding grey depending on the weather.

It was here, during a storm that her foal was born. Billy, the farm labourer was making his way down from working in the hills when he spotted Gypsy amongst the gorse with her new-born foal. Excited that the foal had finally arrived he ran straight to the house calling for John and the family. Debbie was already home from school, so in the stormy weather they all walked up the sheep track. Gypsy was on her feet, proudly showing off her foal who had a dark coat, almost the colour of the black, stormy sky. Debbie named the foal Storm.

At first Storm was quite timid around the family, but eventually his confidence grew and he turned into a cheeky youngster who loved nothing more than running. There was plenty to amuse him on the farm. He would trot up and down neighing to bulls in the next field and would pace after the deer that jumped into his field. Debbie spent a lot of time out in the field getting him used to being handled.

The young girl and foal became firm friends. They would play chase – a game the foal loved, Debbie and Storm would race around after one another. Debbie would hide in the bushes while Storm would prance around until he found her, then he would gallop off with Debbie in pursuit. He would spin around with a playful buck or kick, all the time waiting for her to catch up and then off he would go again at full pace around her. Often he would run up to her then at the last minute he would whip around. He loved to tease and was always trying to claim the upper hand.

Six weeks after his birth Storm travelled with Gypsy back to the stud. This was the first time in the horsebox and he walked in calmly, snuggling up to his mum for reassurance. After a six-week stay at Glenluce, Gypsy was in foal, for a second time to Jay River and returned home with her son.

Storm as a foal with his dark grey coat

When it was time for Storm to be weaned, he was brought to the big barn opposite the farm house, with Pixie and Katie's quiet old pony, Pepe, for company. During the day he was led into a paddock opposite Gypsy's field where he could see his mum, but she soon became less interested in her first born.

Storm's youthful exuberance was tolerated by his more mature companions, as he reared and plunged and galloped around them. Handling him was also quite testing, and he often nearly landed Debbie in a heap with his mischief.

As he matured he began to settle down. By the time Debbie was ready to leave home for university he was fairly docile and could be led in a halter.

Gypsy had a filly foal the following summer and Debbie named her Lady. She looked just like Storm and was dark grey, with a fine thread of silver running through her mane and tail.

Gypsy with her second foal, Storm's full sister, Lady.

With Debbie away at university, Lady didn't get the handling Storm had enjoyed. When the time came to wean the foal, her nature was completely different – she was a stroppy madam with an independent streak. Like a wilful teenager, she did lots of head tossing and stamping if things didn't go her way. Gypsy was a strict mum, and her bossiness seemed to have passed on to her daughter.

When Storm was three years old and his sister was two, there was nothing for them to do other than graze and gallop around their field. The two were quite a handful for the Boams, who were kept busy with farming as well as looking after Katie and her younger brother, Luke.

Lady (on the left) and Storm as youngsters at the Boam family's farm

Debbie with Storm age 3 years old (on the left)
and Lady aged 2 years old.

Katie aged 10 holding Storm for a photo
before he left the farm.

It wasn't long before Storm started to show his jumping ability, easily clearing the walls that surrounded his field, to get to the better grass on the other side. The tough decision was made to sell both youngsters, with the proceeds going towards Debbie's University education.

Miami Mystique

After Storm was sold he was renamed Misty
and acquired his first show name at
Hugh Paterson's Miami Stud.

That autumn a local horse breeder and dealer called John Dunlop was delivering a lorry load of hay to the farm for the sheep. During conversation, while unloading the bales, John Boam mentioned the two young ponies he had for sale. Debbie showed Mr Dunlop the ponies and they agreed a price.

A few days later Mr Dunlop came to collect the youngsters in the horsebox. Storm was trusting and calm and happily went into the horsebox, but his sister, true to form, would not behave. Storm was loaded on and off with the hope that Lady would follow him but to no avail. She did not want to load and eventually had to be unceremoniously man handled into the truck.

At the dealer's yard in Annan the two were handled and taught how to lunge, before being laid off for the winter. In those days, without passports a legal requirement, their original names were forgotten. Storm was renamed Misty and Lady became known as Miracle.

Storm being lead into the horsebox leaving the Boam's farm as a 3 year old. Debbie leading him on and Katie watching.

John Dunlop had a business partner, Hugh Paterson, and together they would go to the horse sales, looking for well-bred young sport horses and ponies. Both men had an interest in showjumping and a good eye for spotting potential.

On one of their trips to Ireland John and Hugh bought a pure-bred Connemara colt foal they spotted trotting down the street with his dam at Ballinasloe fair. They immediately loved the young colt and bought him. John planned to use him at stud since he had very good bloodlines and proved to be a careful jumper. They named that pony Hocki.

In the following spring, Misty and Miracle were sent to Hugh Paterson's farm, where they would be introduced to riding. The two ponies quickly settled into life at Hugh's, a peaceful setting on the Wigtownshire coast. Karen Hutchings, or Missy as her friends knew her, had the task of doing the ground work with the two, introducing them to the saddle and bridle in preparation for being ridden. Misty took to this easily but Miracle had other ideas and rebelled every step of the way against all that was done to her.

Since Miracle proved difficult to handle it was decided she would return to John Dunlop to run with the colt Hocki. She ended up being a very good broodmare for him and had several foals sired by Hocki over the years.

Hugh is not a man for luxuries. Horses are his life and he loves to talk about them. He broke his own horses and well into his 70s would mount the young ones. He has a stall with a feed barrier over the top and he would climb up the step-ladder, hold onto the barrier, put his leg over the horse and hang on (it worked!).

At the entrance to Hugh's farm there is an impressive hawthorn bush that Hugh has skilfully pruned into the shape of a horse's head, complete with a headcollar.

Hugh had been a dairy farmer until the early 1980s and has successfully shown Ayrshire cows, Clydesdales and light horses at every annual Wigtown Agricultural Show since the second World War.

Showing horses at Wigtown is still one of his highlights. He got his first pony when he was eight. "I used to show my ponies and then take part in the gymkhana having hacked them all the way to Wigtown in the morning and then would hack them back home again at night," says Hugh.

At fifteen he helped break in his first horses for Tommy Hanlin and then the Evans family. Hugh worked the land, ploughing with Clydesdale horses and subsequently entered ploughing competitions in his later years. With a lifelong love of horses, he has a wealth of equestrian knowledge and a good eye for a horse.

Hugh's granddaughter, Heather, had inherited his genes and was pony mad. When she was young she had a small palomino mare called Chippie, who she competed. Heather loved Chippie but she became lame and was no longer suitable for her to ride in competitions. Heather was devastated, being without a pony to ride was the worst thing that could happen to her.

Heather was desperate for another pony and wished to compete and ride but her mum and dad had just separated and her dad wasn't keen on the idea. Just to be close to horses, Heather would go and help at the local riding club every weekend. It was small consolation for not having her own pony, but she enjoyed helping put the jumps up and grooming for friends.

As Heather's love for horses showed no sign of waning, her dad eventually came around to the idea of her having another pony of her own. And so began their lengthy search for something suitable. They ended up travelling what seemed like the length and breadth of Scotland looking for a pony, up to 14.2hh, that would be trustworthy enough for Heather to look after on her own at the farm. They were hoping for a schoolmaster, but Heather was tall for her age and finding the perfect pony within their budget was not easy.

Their fruitless search continued until the next time they went to visit Hugh. Heather immediately spotted Misty, the handsome grey standing in one of the stalls. She asked if she could try the pony, but Hugh told them quite adamantly that Misty was too much for Heather, as he had only just been broken in.

Heather's heart sank, Misty looked like a good type of pony, big enough for her to ride, but not too big that she wouldn't be able to handle him. Hugh went on to explain that he could be ridden at walk and trot by a more experienced rider, but wasn't anywhere near ready for a novice.

Heather's dad also liked the look of him and, as Heather says, "Being a farmer he had an eye for a good beast." Using all her powers of persuasion she eventually got Hugh to show them Misty. Hugh put a bridle on and led him out into the yard so that Heather and her dad could look at him properly.

Heather took to Misty immediately. After a saddle was put on, Hugh helped his granddaughter to mount and then sent them round on the lunge rein, getting the pair to walk and trot, just to see how they got on together. Misty behaved impeccably and Heather's dad told Hugh that Misty was the pony for her. He said that if Karen kept schooling him, while allowing Heather to ride him in between, he would eventually be perfect for her.

One day, Hugh took Misty over to Heather's father's farm at Whithorn for a visit, where Karen rode him in the paddock at the front of the farmhouse. She cantered him, for the first time ever, up the hill in the field at the farm. That very same day, Heather hacked her old pony Chippy down the road with Karen riding Misty. Suddenly Misty kicked out at his small companion unfortunately missing his target and catching Heather square on the side of her ankle, breaking a small bone in her foot.

The break, while painful, was also a devastating blow to Heather's plans. While on crutches, not only was she unable to ride, but the accident also meant that she had to miss her Primary seven swimming trip to the Commonwealth pool in Edinburgh.

For a number of months Karen rode Misty to get him going for Heather and then slowly the young pony and his ever-improving rider began to become a team. Misty was taken to his first show as a four-year-old, when Heather was 11. She showed him in the novice pony class and then jumped him in the afternoon. Later the same day her dad bought Misty from Hugh. Heather took him home to be her very own and promised Misty he would never be sold.

It wasn't long before Heather was able to jump Misty in the novice classes at the local Riding Club shows. Back then, Hugh never thought the grey gelding would amount to much, far less become a renowned champion. While Misty showed an aptitude for jumping, his attitude towards his work left much to be desired. In his early days Misty was very green and not the easiest pony to deal with. He refused to load in the horsebox, was difficult to catch, wouldn't stand still to be mounted and continually napped for the gate.

But Heather loved him!

The pair competed for the rest of that year and when the season finished, Misty was turned out for the winter, as there weren't any riding facilities or competitions locally.

The following spring, when Misty was brought back in, he proved to be too much for Heather. She had never had any riding lessons and was still very much a novice rider. Dealing with a wilful five year-old pony, that was slightly big for her, was too much of a challenge.

Help was found in the form of Heather's mum who was now living in Ayrshire. Heather's dad asked if she could take Misty for a couple of weeks, just to get him back into work.

When Misty returned to the farm, the only place to ride was a seven-acre field and while Heather's mum had got Misty going again, he was still a handful for his young rider. Each time he passed the field gate he would start to nap and buck. He had the upper hand in the battle of wills, rolling his eyes back and setting his neck to charge straight for the gate.

There was no one to help her get on him safely, or offer advice when he was a handful to ride. Heather had to do everything herself and found it a real struggle. But that struggle, along with the bumps, the bruises, the falls, the tears and the dramas were nothing compared to how bad she would feel without a pony to ride. If Heather hadn't loved him so much, and been so desperate for a pony, she probably would have given up on him.

Without help Heather had to improvise, she would take him to the nearest dyke and scramble on board because he would not stand still long enough for her to mount in the conventional way. She spent every spare minute she had with Misty and kept riding and riding until eventually he began to realise that she meant business and started to behave.

During their first proper show season together, Heather and Misty competed each week at the local Riding Club doing the novice classes, even managing to be placed on some occasions. Towards the end of the summer they were beginning to gel and jumping in classes with higher fences.

Misty acquired his first 'proper' show name while he was competing with Heather. Hugh had used the prefix 'Miami' on his ponies since the 1980s. John Dunlop, who was Hugh's business partner at the time, used to name his ponies after television shows. It was this that sprung to mind when Hugh was asked to name a pony, he was entering for a competition. He started to say 'Miami

Heather introduced Misty to all the local competitions

Vice', after the television show, but quickly realised 'Vice' might not be a good name for a pony, so he swapped it for 'Maestro'. From that day on, all his ponies had the 'Miami' prefix, usually followed with names beginning with the letter 'M'. Misty became known at local shows as Miami Mystique

Heather's dad was busy on the farm and with her mum not around, it was a struggle for both of them. Misty became Heather's life and they became inseparable. Heather used to sleep in the field with Misty lying beside him in the grass. She would never go on holiday, as she couldn't bear to leave him any more than she had to.

While Misty lived to jump, Heather also won dressage with him, which was a testimony to how much they had learned and improved together. They won best pony and rider show classes and she even dressed him up in a fancy-dress competition one year for the Whithorn Gala Day. Heather and Misty dressed up as the 'bat out of hell'. Heather was the bat with her swirling black cape and Misty was covered head to toe in a black gown with flames up each side.

The costume, which had been borrowed from Heather's cousin who had made it by hand, won them £5 that day. Misty more than added to the overall effect by rearing the whole way through the procession, creating quite a spectacle for the crowds that lined the street.

Hugh helped Heather at shows and at the Riding Club, particularly with the practice fence. By now they were starting to see Misty's true potential, and Hugh would terrify Heather by putting the jumps up really high and begging her to jump them. No matter how big the fence Misty always jumped them – it was the only thing he seemed to enjoy doing. Often, he napped and refused to enter the ring, but as soon as Heather pointed him at a jump, he would jump it.

As Heather got braver they entered Stranraer Agricultural Show's Open pony Jumping class for the first time and won. It was a huge achievement, as they were competing against some of the best unaffiliated pony and rider combinations in South West Scotland.

Heather couldn't believe they had won, she had never dreamed of being able to achieve a win at such a big show. Even Hugh had a tear in his eye. Misty was the fastest jumping pony he had ever seen – the sharper the turn, the better he jumped. He could clear oxers on a diagonal, land, take one stride, turn and jump another, just as big. Misty made turns no one else would even try – he was phenomenal.

It was a combination of Hugh's encouragement to make those turns and Heather having the sheer grit and determination to pull them off, that helped them become local champions. Hugh always took great pride in telling people Misty could "turn on a tanner!"

Just a week later they competed at Wigtown Agricultural Show's Open pony Jumping class. Aged just 13, Heather's most vivid memory of the day is getting her good jumping shirt covered in paint. As a result she had to compete in a t-shirt bought from one of the stalls, with a grey horse motif on the front of it. She also remembered the show as the day she got her face painted at a stall on the show ground.

Wigtown showground is undulating, following the

contours of the hills. Just like at Stranraer Show, Heather and Misty were competing against the older 15- and 16-year-olds on far more experienced ponies over fences up to 110cm. The young Heather was terrified and excited at the same time. Misty and Heather went clear in the first round and made it into the jump-off.

Heather was so determined and really tried her hardest in the jump-off, focusing on her pony's amazing turning ability. Her heart was in her mouth as Misty careered around the massive course. When they left the ring, Heather asked her dad if they had been fast enough and his answer was 'no', he didn't think it was good enough to win. This upset Heather immensely, as she had given it everything she had.

Lyn McKerlie, an older far more experienced rider who Heather looked up to, had competed in the same class. She had jumped really well that day, so Heather thought it a foregone conclusion that the prize was going to her. Then the announcement came over the tannoy system, saying that Heather and Misty were the winners of the class with the fastest time. It was a dream come true for Heather and tears streamed down her face making her face paint run everywhere!

That was the first time Misty competed against the McKerlie family, but it wouldn't be the last. Lyn's nephew, James Smith, went on to compete against Misty in years to come. In 2006, Thomas Whitaker made a dare-devil turn with Misty to win at the Horse of the Year Show, and James Smith was second on his pony Mr Nice Guy.

Heather with Misty and Katie with Gypsy meeting up at a local show, the ponies recognised each other.

By now, Katie had started competing Gypsy and had many successes in local showjumping competitions. Katie dreamed of competing at Horse of the Year Show after the family went to watch at Wembley Arena in 1996. They started to compete in a few affiliated jumping classes, but it was quite a distance to travel.

Katie recalls: "Gyspy was so reliable and absolutely loved to jump, she always tried her best, we had a lot of fun together. At some local competitions, we met up with Heather who was riding Misty. We were in the 13.2hh jumping class and Heather and Misty were in the 14.2hh jumping class".

"It was lovely to let Gypsy and Misty sniff noses as they recognised each other, arched their necks and whinnied," says Katie. "It was a fun time and brings back a lot of fond memories."

With his ambitious younger daughter in mind, John tried to buy Misty back as Katie was fast outgrowing Gypsy. However, Misty was already making his mark in showjumping and the price reflected his talent, which was more than Katie's dad could afford to pay.

Heather and Misty won all the local showjumping trophies including the Machar's Riding Club points three years in a row. They won just about every other show, too, when Heather's dad could be persuaded to take her further afield.

Losing did not happen very often. A 21-year-old beat them once, after she lied about her age so she could compete in the juniors. While on another occasion Misty spooked at the sight of eight enormous Clydesdales

Miami Bound

The Making of a Champion

In the autumn of 1998 Alan Fazakerley bought Misty from Hugh. Alan met Hugh while he was in Scotland visiting the Steel's who he knew from the showjumping circuit. The Steel's had worked for leading show-jumpers in the past and moved to Scotland to breed competition horses. Alan was always looking for good young horses and ponies and they suggested he go to Hugh's farm and see what he had available, as he was only three miles up the road from them.

Alan is well known in the showjumping world. He has jumped to Grand Prix level and in 1986 won the Puissance at Horse of the Year Show on a horse called Rebound. He is now a highly acclaimed showjumping coach, who has trained the British Pony team to win gold medals in European team and individual events. In 2011 he was named British Showjumping Coach of the Year.

It was some time after his visit that Hugh phoned Alan to say he had a pony that would win the Foxhunter final at the Horse of the Year Show. Alan, who lives near Manchester, didn't meet Misty on his first visit, but he trusted Hugh's judgement and agreed to meet half way to pick him up.

Once in Manchester, Alan could see Misty had great potential, even though at that stage he had not competed under British Showjumping rules.

"I liked him because he was super careful and had a big heart," said Alan, "I thought he was a bit small, but he made up for that. He was quick thinking, nimble and fast and I agreed with Hugh he was going to be a winner, at whatever level he was at."

It wasn't long before Alan sold Misty to the Squibb family where he would acquire his new name. Lauley was in her final year of riding in the 138cm showjumping category, so her family were on the look out to find a 148cm pony for her to produce. At the time they knew Alan and he had invited them to look at Misty and another pony at his yard.

The Squibb family's involvement with horses goes back to Lauley's grandfather, Harry Squibb. He started a business in East London after the Second World War, clearing wreckage and materials away from the Docklands with his horse and cart. The business has grown and is now the leading demolition company in the UK, known as Squibb Group. Lauley's father, Les, is chairman and the company is British Showjumping's longest running sponsor.

Les and his wife, Pat, have been fundamental in supporting the Pony Foxhunter competition, which has hundreds of preliminary rounds held throughout the UK each year. In the summer, there are around ten secondary qualifying rounds with the top two places qualifying for the prestigious final at the Horse of the Year Show.

Horse of the Year Show, or HOYS at it is commonly known, is where all showjumpers aspire to compete. It is the pinnacle of the season, where children and professionals alike dream of riding under the magical spotlights, signifying they have won at 'the world's most famous horse show'.

Les has a passion for showjumping and, although he didn't compete, his son rode and Lauley has achieved great success in the sport. Les and Pat's connection with horses and showjumping is strong to this day, with many of their grandchildren competing in affiliated classes. Les has supported the Pony Foxhunter Championship since 1997. He takes great pleasure in seeing pony riders go onto achieve success on horses at senior level and is clearly delighted to sponsor a series that provides such an important foundation for the sport.

One of Lauley's first showjumping ponies was a super 128cm pony called Metric. He and Lauley were consistently in the top placings at all the big equestrian centres in England in the 128cm JA category, from when she was just ten years old. Metric was a special jumping pony, who gave several top riders their first taste of national showjumping success from 1987 right up until 2006.

As well as Metric, Lauley had formed a successful partnership with the 138cm jumping pony Ferry Bound. They won all of Britain's major shows for 138cm pony's including placings at HOYS. Lauley was clearly a very talented and competitive rider and worked hard to be the best she could be. Showjumping was a family affair, and

Claire Squibb played a key role in looking after the ponies, turning them out immaculately and organising them behind the scenes. Will Bound was another pony who Lauley brought on through the grades, from British Novice to being placed in both the Pony Newcomers and Pony Foxhunter finals at HOYS in 1998.

When the Squibb's tried Misty they stayed at Alan's for a couple of days in Manchester. Lauley and Claire instantly liked the dapple grey pony, even before he had been ridden. Unfortunately, that first ride did not go well. Such was Misty's cheeky streak that he ran out at the first cross pole he was asked to jump. However, the girls were used to ponies and knew instinctively that this was not real naughtiness, he was just testing out his rider.

Both Lauley and her father had a good feeling about Misty, and knew enough about ponies to understand all the best ones have funny quirks. Once Misty realised Lauley was a confident rider, the rest of the trial went well.

Their gut feeling turned out to be right. Misty would go on to forge a special partnership with the family. Alan asked them to keep the pony's Miami prefix for his affiliated name and the Squibb's tagged on 'Bound', in the hope he would be as good as Lauley's previous pony, Ferry Bound.

Once the deal was done and they were about to leave, Misty was bandaged in preparation for the journey home. The girls went to say goodbye to Alan and when they returned to the stable he had taken his bandages off. His strong, mischievous character was a constant source of amusement, as Claire remembers.

"He was a real character and took his bandages off any chance he could in the beginning," Claire says. "Each time he was loaded on to the lorry he charged up the ramp into the truck and charged straight out again, like a train. He was so strong you couldn't hold him when he pulled, and he liked to do things his way. In the end you just had to laugh at him!"

The Squibbs worked hard to get the best out of Misty, despite his antics. There were a few challenges with him at the start, but their experience was instrumental in bringing out the best in him.

Lauley took the newly named Miami Bound up through the grades of affiliated jumping in copy book style. They started out in January 1999 and won most of their competitions. By March they had four double clears in the Blue Chip Junior Newcomers classes, having won two of them, qualifying them for the second rounds. Lauley's experience significantly benefited Misty, giving him confidence and guidance around the more technical affiliated courses. A calm and proficient rider, Lauley made all their rounds look easy and their results were so consistent, they rarely had any faults.

The partnership stepped up to jumping in what was then called the 'Squibb and Davis Junior Foxhunter' classes (the contest sponsored by Lauley's family) and within a short time had qualified for second rounds. Incredibly they were placed in every second round competition they did, which consisted of three rounds of jumping, with the jumps getting bigger each time.

In June they were third in the Pony Foxhunter second

round at South View Equestrian Centre. To contest three rounds against fierce competition, over the biggest track Misty had faced, was a huge achievement considering they had only been together six months.

That autumn they competed in a major championship at the Festival of Showjumping. It was Misty's biggest class to date, but he seemed unfazed by all the decorations on the jumps and didn't spook at any of the fillers.

Claire Squibb recalls some memories from the championship shows, where they had to stay overnight in temporary stables.

"Misty was put in the stable at night and in the morning he was gone," she says. "He could let himself out and spend the night standing outside a pony mates stable. Whilc hc was naughty, thcrc was nevcr any badness in him and his antics always made us laugh."

When Lauley had a number of ponies at a show the girls would tie them up on the side of the lorry while they went to jump. When they came back he would always have untied himself and be grazing. He never went far from the lorry, just to the nearest patch of tasty grass.

By the end of the season in 1999, Lauley and Misty had achieved all their double clears, ready to contest second rounds for Pony Newcomers and Pony Foxhunter qualifiers in 2000. That itself is an incredible achievement.

Misty was proving to be a very reliable and capable affiliated jumping pony. Lauley's experience played a key part in his development from jumping unaffiliated tracks with Heather, to tackling wider, technical affiliated tracks in daunting championship arenas. It was clear he loved his job; he always had his ears pricked looking at a jump no matter how big or frightening it was.

The year 2000 was Lauley's last year of jumping Misty, as she would turn 16 and was therefore no longer eligible to compete in pony classes. Her ambition was to qualify for the championships at HOYS, held at Wembley Arena in London.

They had stepped up to Junior Members Cup competitions with a good win at Arena UK in January and another big win at the Pony of the Year show in April. This was followed by more good results in junior open competitions in preparation for second round qualifiers.

Hundreds of young riders are in these second round competitions, all dreaming of a place at HOYS, but only the top two combinations go through. Just to qualify is an achievement and getting it right on the day is not easy under immense pressure. The second round tracks are often bigger and more technical than the finals.

While Misty could be lazy at home, he always enjoyed being at a show. The bigger the atmosphere the better he performed. When Lauley introduced him to water trays, which he didn't like, rather than stop he was more likely to jump higher.

Misty rarely let anyone down, but there was one occasion when things did not go according to plan. The Squibbs had travelled all the way to Bold Heath in Lancashire for one of the second round competitions, but when they arrived something was clearly wrong. Misty did not look well. There was no choice but to stay the night and the following morning they went home.

He was put out into the field where he lay down, eating the grass. This was completely out of character so they knew something was very wrong. The vet was called and blood tests confirmed he had a virus, which was devastating news for the Squibbs as the second round competitions were starting. Thankfully, he recovered just in time to be back in work a week before the HOYS qualifiers.

Lauley and Miami Bound went on to win two of the main classes at Lordsbridge's two-day show in Cambridgeshire: the JA/JC handicap and the Blue Chip Junior Newcomers HOYS qualifier, which guaranteed them a place in the final at Wembley. Two weeks later they travelled to a show in Lincolnshire and came second in the Squibb and Davis Junior Foxhunter second round, which meant they had two HOYS tickets! These results were an outstanding achievement considering the hundreds of ponies who compete for a qualifying place at the prestigious show.

The combination had continued success that summer in junior open classes with placings at major venues including Wales & West and Hickstead. The final show before HOYS was the Festival of Showjumping at Arena UK in Lincolnshire. Lauley had set her sights on the Squibb and Davis Junior Foxhunter Masters championship, held on the final day of the six-day festival. There were two preliminary rounds to qualify for the final and Lauley and Miami Bound made it through to the championship with ease.

The Foxhunter Masters' championship course was set up in the decorated indoor arena and was contested over three rounds. Those clear after jumping two rounds would go into a final round, against the clock. By the time the jump off started, quite a crowd had gathered to watch. Lauley remembers going so fast and feeling like she was literally flying over the fences.

Lauley Squibb and Miami Bound won the Squibb and Davies Junior Foxhunter Masters

“I remember turning to a big oxer and Misty just going higher,” Lauley says. “It was such an amazing feeling, he was unbelievable!.”

They set a remarkable time that proved unbeatable and won the competition.

They posed for photos before a well-deserved lap of honour, cheered on by all Lauley's friends and family and the delighted crowd. The dapple grey looked every bit the champion – plaited up and covered in a sash and rosettes as they paraded around the arena to loud applause.

Lauley's mother, Pat, awarded their first prize along with a sash, rosettes and a silver cup.

The pair were so hard to beat they were favourite to win the Squibb and Davies Junior Foxhunter final at HOYS. Given the family connection, this was one competition that Lauley really wanted to win. However, things did not quite go to plan and they finished the class with four faults, to finish eighth. Although this was still a credible achievement it was disappointing for Lauley, as she really wanted to win at HOYS. This was her final competition with Misty and she had one more championship, the Blue Chip Junior Newcomers final, which would be the very last time they competed together.

Misty must have felt Lauley's determination and it's almost like he knew what he had to do. After a foot perfect clear in the first round of the competition, Lauley decided to go for it in the jump off aiming for the fastest round possible leaving the jumps up. Misty turned and jumped at speed and tucked up his legs, thrilling the crowd as they crossed the finish, seconds ahead of the other competitors. The commentator gave a big cheer and said, "Wow what a round Lauley! Can anyone else get near that time?".

Their round proved to be unbeatable and ensured a win in the HOYS Blue Chip Junior Newcomers Final. After being so disappointed at having a pole down in the Foxhunter Final it was remarkable that they came back fighting and fulfilled Lauley's lifelong dream of winning at HOYS.

Misty and Lauley were presented with a rug and sash, and escorted into the packed Wembley Arena under spot lights, alongside two mounted drummers of the household cavalry. It was a moment Lauley will never forget. Misty seemed to enjoy every moment of the presentation, too. He stood proud, ears pricked, and looked stunning as the photographers flashed their cameras for a picture, which would appear in *Horse and Hound* magazine.

Lauley knew the show would be her last as she had

decided not to go onto horses at the same level. "I feel so proud, now more than ever, of what Misty and I achieved together," she fondly recalls. "We had a special bond, for sure."

Lauley sobbed uncontrollably when they won at HOYS, the mixture of emotions too much for a young girl to keep in. She was so happy they got to finish on a high.

"I was glad we did it together, you can't get better than winning a final at the Horse of the Year Show at Wembley," she says. "It was sad as I knew my journey with him had come to an end, but we had so much fun."

"I feel privileged to have had him and proud that I was a part of his amazing career. The more you asked, the better Misty got. He never said no, or I can't. Ponies like him are so hard to find. Lucky for me my dad had a good eye for picking ponies. I appreciate that now, more than ever.

Claire also has fond, proud memories of their time with this showjumping superstar, and says they "loved every minute of him".

"I don't remember him ever letting us down," she says. "If he was older we probably would have kept him, but he was too young and he wasn't happy doing nothing. He was born to be a star, a true performer with true grit, courage, skill, talent and that 'all knowing ' look in his eye. It was a privilege to have him in our stable. Lauley and Misty learned so much together and achieved so much."

After Lauley stopped competing Miami Bound at the end of 2000, the Squibbs were keen to see how he would cope competing against the JA ponies in 148cm Championship classes. Misty had already shown promise of being a big track pony with Lauley, the tracks in theses competitions are around 1.30m high.

There were some remarkable ponies competing during the 2000 and 2001 season, who have earned their place as pony showjumping legends. Names such as Colton Maelstrom, New York Spritzer, Gold Harvest and CJ's Kemosabi. There were many others, but these names stand out because they have repeatedly won at the top, with a number of junior riders, over many years.

Horse of the Year Show Champions Lauley Squibb and Miami Bound. Photo by Anthony Reynolds LMPA

Leading Pony Showjumper

Holding his own among the very best
148cm jumping ponies

The Squibb family asked fourteen-year-old Ellen Whitaker to take over the ride on Miami Bound. Ellen is the daughter of Steven, himself an expert horseman and brother to international showjumping riders John and Michael.

The Squibbs were friends with the Whitakers and knew Ellen was a talented and hardworking young rider. She started riding before she could walk and was competing in affiliated showjumping classes from a very early age.

The Horse of the Year Show was a family affair for Ellen, who grew up watching her uncles, John and Michael, compete there. The first time she qualified herself, Ellen was just eight years old! According to Ellen there is nothing like jumping in front of a home crowd and HOYS is the show everyone wants to do well at.

In 2000, Ellen was fifth place in the Leading Pony Showjumper of the Year final at HOYS with Current Ruella, a credit to her talent as she had only been riding the pony for a few months. At that time Ellen still had two more years to compete in pony classes and had a few other good ponies to ride.

Ellen's partnership with Misty began in spring 2001, after a well-earned rest following his win with Lauley at HOYS. They quickly hit it off and had the opportunity to compete in Le Toupuet in France, when Ellen was selected to compete as part of the Accenture Junior International Squad. The pair won classes against some of the leading ponies on the European showjumping circuit, including the prolific European Gold medal winning pony Colton Maelstrom.

Colton Maelstrom and Martha Beaumont were one of many top combinations in the UK at that time. Other great partnerships were New York Spritzer and Louise Pavitt, Gold Harvest and Lance Whitehouse, and CJ's Kemosabi and Stacy Jefferies. These pony legends had already proven themselves and Miami Bound was now holding his own among them. Ellen and Miami Bound accumulated many wins and top placings, including a win in the Leading Pony Showjumper of the Year qualifier at Devon County Show, fulfilling what the Squibb's had believed he was capable of.

The Leading Pony Showjumper of the Year Championship has been hugely popular since the first HOYS in 1949. In 1953, 175 ponies were entered for the class, which would have been a marathon to watch and taken most of the day. These days the qualifying rounds are tough and places in the final are limited to 25 combinations of pony and rider. Competitors must qualify for the final by achieving a place in the top three of regional preliminary rounds.

The final at HOYS reaches a height of 1.45m, which is the biggest class for ponies in Europe, if not the world.

Most European Pony Championships in recent years reach a maximum height of 1.35m.

Less than two weeks after Ellen and Misty won the regional qualifier at Devon, they travelled to the four-day junior festival at Hickstead. Out of four JA competitions they won one, came second twice and took fifth place in another. The usual rivals were Colton Maelstrom who picked up a second place with Martha Beaumont; Louise Pavitt and New York Spritzer, who had a great show winning three of their classes; and Gold Harvest with Lance Whitehouse taking good placings. These ponies seemed to take it in turns to inhabit the top spots of all the premier pony competitions that season.

The next competition after Hickstead was the Scope Festival of Showjumping at the end of August. It's a prestigious six-day festival with an atmospheric indoor arena at Stafford County show ground. Along with all the other leading junior riders, Ellen had her sights set on the £1000 prize which would go to the winner of the Dunglenn 148cm Championship.

Ellen qualified for the Championship by coming third in the preliminary round, held on the first day of the show. New York Spritzer and Louise Pavitt were favourites for the final after winning both preliminary rounds. The Championship was held on the final evening of the show and provided a fitting climax for Britain's best under-16 riders. Spectators had gathered around the arena and balcony in good spirits to watch, including many of the UK's top senior showjumpers, who were competing at the show.

Ellen and Miami Bound made the first round look easy, even though the jumps were massive. They produced a lovely clear, with Misty stretching out over the wide oxers and combination fences, making it through into the jump-off where the fences would go up even higher.

Ellen was drawn second to go in the jump off and knew she had to go fast and clear to have a chance of winning. They took on the track with speed and determination and after an impressive tight turn to the third fence the crowd really got behind them with cheers of 'Go on Ellen' making the round even more exciting.

Despite a slip going into the penultimate upright, Ellen navigated an almost impossible turn to the last fence, a big and wide oxer, Miami Bound answered with an almighty leap, tucking up his feet after barely seeing it before him, saving every fraction of a second. It was a spectacular round and the crowd went wild in appreciation with cheers and applause.

Misty seemed to revel in the ovation and Ellen gave him a big pat hoping it would be enough to secure them first place. The round proved difficult to beat and only Louise and New York Spritzer could get close. They went around with a super-fast clear, although they didn't take the turn to the last fence Ellen had dared, which meant they were a few hundredths of a second slower. Ellen and Miami Bound had won! It was one of Ellen's biggest wins in her pony career and all her family where there to watch and celebrate the occasion as she was awarded a sash and the £1000 first prize.

Ellen Whitaker with Miami Bound en route to a terrific Dunglenn 148cm Championship victory at Scope Festival of Showjumping 2001

The next competition was the Arena UK Festival of Showjumping, where junior and senior competitors from all over the UK compete in the last major Championships before HOYS. Ellen came away with one good win and a credible ninth place in two of the open classes. This was the same venue where Miami Bound had won the Junior Foxhunter Masters the previous year with Lauley Squibb.

Soon it was October and the pinnacle of the season – Horse of the Year Show at London's Wembley Arena. The Leading Pony Showjumper of the Year final would take place on Sunday, which was one of the busiest days of the show. In 2001 the class was sponsored by Paul Fabrications. This was the class Ellen wanted to win.

Despite the packed arena, you could hear a pin drop as the crowd didn't want to distract the ponies or riders as they tackled the huge, tough course. There were only a few clear rounds when Ellen and Misty went in. They jumped the first round in front of the hushed crowd, who let out a big cheer as they crossed the finish clear and together they had made it look so easy.

When they went into the jump off they knew what they had to do, Martha Beaumont had set the standard with a very fast clear on the legendary pony Colton Maelstrom, who had won the title previously in 1997 and 1999.

Ellen went in and they seemed to fly around the enormous jumps, which were now up to 1.45m. Up on the clock, the crowd were behind them, willing them on. It looked like they would do it, until the last line of jumps where Miami Bound rubbed the front pole of an oxer going into the final double, for four faults. It was still good enough for second place as the fastest round with only Martha going clear in the jump off. Ellen and Misty proudly rode into the arena under the spotlights for the presentation and a well-earned standing ovation from the crowd.

The other placings that year went to Meadowcroft Minstrel ridden by Leanne Riley who came third and they had also been third place in the same class in 1999. Fourth spot went to the famous coloured cob CJ's Kemosabi ridden by Stacy Jefferies. CJ's Kemosabi won the title the following year, 2002, with Andrew Mizon and again in 2004 with Louise Saywell.

This was an amazing achievement for Miami Bound's first season, competing against the top JA ponies, some of which he would face again in 2006 with Ellen's brother Tom.

Although the Squibbs loved Misty and were thrilled with his achievements with Ellen, they decided to sell him on at the end of 2001. He was too young to retire and he would be able to go on and give another young rider a lot of fun. Ellen's last competition with him was at Southview Equestrian in October where they won the top JA class in the climax of the show.

Ellen's brother Joe briefly took over the ride on Miami Bound at the end of the year and was placed in an Open class at Talk of the North Equestrian Centre in November, before he was sold to Nicola Fitzgibbon in Ireland.

Bound for Ireland

A new life competing against the best ponies in Ireland

Miami Bound was advertised in the prestigious *Horse and Hound*, where the advert was seen by Nicola FitzGibbon's mother Kathryn. She was, as Nicola's father says: "The main dynamo in the family when it came to ponies for Nicola and she monitored everything that was for sale in England and Ireland."

Nicola at that stage was a talented and competitive young rider, keen to progress from her 138cm jumping pony Kiltullas King.

Miami Bound was clearly a very capable pony, but as he wasn't as expensive as a top grade pony, Nicola's parents felt they wouldn't lose money on him, even if he didn't click with their daughter. The only negative they could see was that since Miami Bound had been ridden by Ellen Whitaker, taking the ride over from her wasn't necessarily going to be straight forward. Ellen might be able to get an awful lot more out of a pony than an average rider.

At the time, Nicola had only been competing for around a year and was lucky to have parents keen to help her. She first had riding lessons at the age of eight at Spruce Lodge, run by Joan Keogh, where she learnt the basics, along with stable management.

After months of saving up and doing odd jobs she got her first pony Copper. He taught Nicola the art of staying on, among other things, and they had great fun in the Kilternan, Bray and Kildare Hunt Pony Clubs. When it became obvious Nicola was not going to tire of riding, her parents bought Kiltullas King, a competitive 138cm Connemara jumping pony.

It was with Kiltullas King that Nicola gained experience jumping big courses and competed as a member of Showjumping Ireland (SJI), the Irish equivalent to British Showjumping. They had a successful partnership and came second place in the 138cms Championship at the Royal Dublin Society (RDS) Dublin Horse Show. That was a major achievement since Nicola was relatively inexperienced at that level.

The week of Dublin Horse Show was the most exciting week of the year for Nicola, she had been a spectator at the show as a child and was inspired by watching all the leading senior riders.

The RDS Dublin Horse Show is a celebration of Ireland's affinity with the horse, from the best show horses to top international showjumpers. It is one of Ireland's largest events and attracts tens of thousands of people from all over the world. The show has one of the largest annual prize pots for international Showjumping in the world and features the Nations Cup Competition for the Aga Khan Trophy, part of the FEI Nations Cup Series. The leading 128cm, 138cm and 148cm ponies must qualify to attend, and then qualify at the show in preliminary rounds to compete in the championship.

Showjumping became a way of life for Nicola and her family. Her success on Kiltullas King encouraged Nicola to progress, hence the search for a second, bigger pony.

In the autumn of 2001 the FitzGibbon family travelled to Southview Equestrian Centre in Cheshire after arranging to view Miami Bound. They watched from the side-lines as Misty won the JA class with Ellen Whitaker. Once the competition had wrapped up for the evening Nicola tested him out.

Things did not go well, as Nicola recalls: "I remember it all very well as embarrassingly, I managed to fall off at a 1m fence while trying him. It was made even worse by the fact that a lot of the riders had gathered at the arena to watch me!"

Misty had been jumping up to 1.35m in the class, but when it was time for Nicola to try him the Whitakers put the jumps down. Whether the double striding was now wrong for the short striding pony, or he just jumped too big, Nicola fell off. Luckily she was unharmed, except for a dented pride.

Undeterred they went back to try him at another show, where fortunately the trial went much better and shortly after that he arrived at the FitzGibbon's yard. Nicola knew that he was a super smart pony who absolutely loved his job, but even so, as she recalls "I knew that Ellen would be a hard act to follow."

Nicola had trouble clicking with Misty at first, which she modestly puts down to a lack of experience. Her parents didn't put any pressure on Nicola to do well, but she felt frustrated, knowing how expensive Misty had been and how good he had been with Ellen.

Help came in the form of Derek Black, a trainer from England, who had helped the family buy a previous pony. He flew over every week for a few weeks and taught Nicola how to ride Misty. He quickly and correctly assessed she was trying too hard.

"He taught me to just sit there – it was very simple really," Nicola explains. "I was trying to do too much. Sit there, take my leg off and point the pony at the fence – not too complicated."

To everyone's delight, it wasn't long before they began to achieve the success they had hoped for. Nicola and Misty won their first 148cm grade A class in February and for the next few months they competed in all the major 148cm pony competitions throughout Ireland.

"If I hadn't clicked with him it would have been the end of ponies for me for sure – we weren't in the position to go out and buy a string of top ponies," says Nicola.

Nicola's determination and hard work in training paid off and the pair qualified for the 148cm jumping class at the RDS Dublin Horse Show in early August. Nicola really wanted to do well in front of the Irish crowds and the international riders, who she looked up to.

In the preliminary round, Nicola guided Misty round the huge course of jumps, which proved to be particularly challenging, causing most ponies to have faults. They had just one down, but were the fastest four faults to come second. This meant they were guaranteed a place in the final at the weekend, giving Misty two days to recover.

While many of the top junior riders are very focussed on one particular competition, Nicola and her Mum were far more relaxed in their approach.

"We were so ignorant about the competitions that we tootled along and did our own thing," Nicola recalls with a smile.

Doing her own thing meant that Nicola was also riding her other pony in a showing class at the Dublin Horse Show, which happened to be on the same day as the 148cm Championship. She won her showing class and then had to wait for the showing championship, where she was awarded reserve champion with her 138cm show pony Kennilwood Pushkin.

After the showing championship, Nicola had to trot through the crowded showground up to Simmonscourt, where the jumping classes were held. Since they had been so busy with the showing, she hadn't had chance to groom Misty properly. Nicola was aware of quizzical looks from the 'proper showjumpers,'

"People were like, 'who's this girl with the scruffy pony?'," Nicola laughs.

But in true pony fiction style Nicola and her "scruffy pony" went on to jump two incredible clear rounds and win the 148cm Championship class, which that year was shown live on Irish television.

Some of the world's top showjumpers sit on the side-lines to watch the pony championships, along with the Irish President and many other dignitaries that are present. In the vast main arena, jumping huge fences in front of the crowds, would put pressure on any rider, but Miami

Nicola FitzGibbon and Miami Bound RHS Dublin Horse Show 148cm winner. Photo by Tony Parkes Photographer

Bound and Nicola were so determined, their jump-off time was over two seconds faster than nearest rivals Antony Condon and Another Riot.

After their huge success at Dublin, a few weeks later they went on to win two SJAI National Championship titles at Goffs equestrian centre, both the Gain Feeds 148A and 148 ABC Speed Championship. By the end of the 2002 season, Nicola and Miami Bound had won the three most prestigious classes for 148cm jumping ponies in Ireland.

Their achievements were celebrated at The Showjumpers Awards Ball at the end of the year, a black-tie event to celebrate the very best of showjumping. Awards are given to champion riders, owners of horses who have achieved brilliance, and even the grooms who look after the horses.

Because of her unprecedented success with Miami Bound, Nicola collected her award for the National 148cm Champion in front of a huge audience. The proud young girl made her way through the tables, packed with all her heroes from the world of showjumping, to stand on the stage and receive the award. Everyone was extremely proud of what they had achieved together.

At the start of the following season in 2003, Nicola was in her last year of riding ponies and aimed for a place on the pony Nations Cup and European teams later that year. To gain experience competing abroad, Nicola and her family, along with a few other young Irish riders, travelled to an FEI (Fédération Equestre Internationale) competition in Diest, Belgium. Nicola and Miami Bound managed to win the pony Grand Prix against some of the best combinations in Europe. They then travelled to

Fontainebleau, France and achieved a credible third place in the pony Grand Prix there.

The year 2003 was very competitive for Irish pony riders, who had dominated the placings abroad. So to be selected for the Nations Cup team to compete at CSIOP Freudenberg Germany was a great achievement. Nicola and Miami Bound made the Irish team selection along with their usual rivals; Anthony Condon riding Mister Polo Bear, Mark Flynn riding Kilcannon Explosion and Mark McAuley riding Shalom Outlaw.

For the Nations Cup they would all do their best for each other and after two rounds of jumping they were the only team to finish with no faults, which was good enough to win the team competition, knocking Great Britain into second place. All the Irish competitors and their families were incredibly emotional about the win, proud of their ponies and how well they had done against leading teams from all over Europe. It was an amazing experience for them all to stand on the podium ahead of the Great Britain and German teams.

There was nothing Misty wasn't good at and because of the pair's relative inexperience in showjumping he was entered into every kind of competition. They did the Puissance, Six Bar and the Millstreet Derby, plus all sorts of speed classes and soon discovered Misty would do anything that was asked of him.

As Nick, Nicola's father, says: "It just shows what a great pony he was that he gave Nicola the experience she needed and was good enough to take a relatively inexperienced rider and bring her to the top."

The Six Bar competition is where ponies jump a row of six fences in a straight line. If any of the fences are knocked down the rider is out. After each round the fences are put up and the process is repeated.

In the final round of the Six Bar at Cavan Equestrian Centre, the last of the six jumps was a 1.65m upright, with three poles at the top and a big space at the bottom, which the ponies could have ridden under. Miami Bound loved to jump and it didn't seem to matter how high the jumps were, he gave them his best attempt and sailed over the final fence. He was the only pony to jump all six without any faults and won the class. They also won a two-fence challenge at Cavan clearing two uprights at a height of 1.70m!

In the Puissance competition there are two jumps, a large spread jump and then a large solid wall made up of lightweight wooden bricks painted red. Each time a pony jumped clear the crowd would cheer them on and the jumps would go up. Nicola and Misty kept going clear, making it look easy as the other competitors had faults and were eliminated.

The wall got up to an impressive 1.75m causing great excitement. Cheers and applause followed when Nicola and Misty jumped it clear. Only one other, Antony Condon and his pony Mr Polar Bear had made it that far. The final round went up to a daunting 1.85m.

Nicola and Misty jumped the huge spread jump first, which had also gone up to around 1.50m and after it they had a good stride to the wall, giving it everything but Misty's stifle nudged the top ever so slightly and the top tile fell, but what an attempt. They were both extremely brave to take on such a fence and the crowd was thrilled. After the competition, all the young riders who had been watching walked into the arena and stood near the wall, awe-struck at how big and imposing the jump was. Such courage pony and rider would have needed to attempt it.

One major disappointment for Nicola was the European Championships, in Necarne, Ireland – something she blames on her own nerves. In the two team trials, they finished second and first, and were the only combination to jump two clear rounds. Misty was easily the smallest and probably the only genuine pony competing. But unfortunately, nerves got to Nicola and in the opening competition things went wrong. Nicola was uptight and they didn't jump brilliantly. Based on that one round, she was left out of the team, which eventually consisted of Anthony and Claire Condon, Mark Flynn and Mark McCauley.

When they weren't competing Nicola would take Miami Bound out onto the Curragh, a huge open plain near where they lived in Co Kildare. It was home to many of the best racehorse training stables and also the Curragh Camp, where the Irish Defence Forces train. Here they could gallop around the vast open land and canter up and down the shooting butts. Misty absolutely loves to gallop, so it must have been a tremendous thrill for them both. After all, Misty has racing genes in his blood.

Towards the end of the season, the Showjumping Ireland National Championships were once again held at Goffs in August 2003. Nicola was as determined as ever to do well, especially since this would be the final few competitions she would have with Miami Bound. They managed to retain their 148cm National Championship title for the second year running, jumping clear in a competitive jump off with an unbeatable time.

Over the next few weeks they went on to win both the Millstreet Pony Owners Grand Prix and the Portalaoise Grand Prix, which ended their partnership on a high.

Nicola was destined to be one of Ireland's leading lady riders and the move on to horses was exciting for her, but it was tough to say goodbye to the ponies she had worked so hard with and learnt so much from. Miami Bound was advertised for sale and with his record of championship wins it was not difficult to find him a new home, with another up-and-coming young rider.

"Nicola's mother Kathryn had put together a wonderful video of his competition highlights to advertise him and she kindly sent a copy of the tape to us," recalls breeder, John Boam. "She was interested to hear that we still had Misty's mother, Gypsy, and had sent a Christmas card, which we kept safe along with the tape.

"Heather and Hugh also managed to get a copy, which was so precious for us all to have. It has been hidden away like a treasure for years, a special memento of Gypsy's first born. Little did we know then he would make it back to us for retirement. It was difficult to keep track of how he was getting on, but we all knew he would be sold to a good home. No one would pay a good price for a pony and not treat them well."

When Misty was sold at Christmas, Nicola and her

family went to a show in the Netherlands and bought her first horse, the brilliant Puissance. Several years later in 2011, Nicola would compete on Puissance in the Aga Khan trophy at the RDS Dublin Horse Show.

"Luckily, we bought Puissance as a 7 year old in my first year out of ponies and with hard work and determination he turned into a horse-version of Misty, eventually jumping at five-star Grand Prix level. It's all thanks to those two wonder ponies that I managed to make a career out of showjumping, which I never dreamed I would be able to do."

Nicola will always be thankful to Misty for helping start her career.

"He holds a special place – definitely – without him I don't think I would have progressed to where I am now," she says. "Thanks to all the experience I gained with him at European shows I really got a taste for showjumping.

A new life in Italy, a long way from home

Miami Bound was sold from Ireland to Italy and travelled to numerous European Championships

Orsola Baggio and Miami Bound competing successfully in the 1.35m Grand Prix CSIOP in Belgium, May 2005. Photo by Maud Le Bel photographer of Studforlife.

After the sale of Miami Bound had been agreed, he was bound for Italy to a young rider called Orsola Baggio.

Understandably, it was difficult to keep updated on how he was getting on, so we only know a little about his time there. The partnership didn't 'click' early on, so they contacted Nicola for advice. She recommended the new owners talk to Steven Whitaker, as he knew the pony so well. So they got in touch with him and he was able to help.

John says: "We didn't know when we might see or hear of Misty again, but managed to find a few results and pictures from an internet search. By now Katie was at university, after spending time working as a groom for showjumper Geoff Billington. She had been able to look after and ride Geoff's former Olympic horse It's Otto in his retirement, which was a real privilege, especially as she had posters of the horse on her bedroom wall growing up. Debbie was working full time as a Biology teacher, so our lives were not so involved with the pony show-jumping world."

Misty and Orsola had a few good results in Grand Prix classes and were part of the Italian Pony Showjumping European team, with their best individual results in Belgium (CSIO Poney de Moorsele) and France (Fontainebleau).

Misty's passport has fourteen FEI stamps from his time in Italy, from January 2004 to March 2006. Most are from prestigious equestrian centres around Italy, but there is also one from Austria, one from Belgium and two stamps from Fontainebleau, France. He was certainly well travelled.

It is possible Misty had some time off due to an

injury, since he has quite a big scar on his forearm, clearly showing where stiches would have been. It's not certain how, or when, this happened, but it would seem he lost some confidence jumping while in Italy. Or perhaps Orsola was not as competitive as his former riders. Maybe we will find out more one day.

A welcome return to the Whitakers yard in Yorkshire

In the early spring of 2006, Orsola's family contacted Steven Whitaker

After Orsola had grown out of Miami Bound, her family contacted Steven Whitaker, since he had been a help to their partnership at the beginning. Steven knew what a good pony Miami Bound was and thought he'd be perfect for his son, Thomas, who at fifteen, had one year left to compete on ponies. Tom had been a competitive young rider on smaller ponies, so Steven knew he would be able to get Misty back to his best.

Tom had fond memories of the super grey pony that his sister Ellen had done so well on, so knowing he was going to ride Miami Bound was an exciting prospect.

"I knew him from Ellen so was very excited when I was told he was coming back," says Tom. "At the time I was the only pony rider in the family, so I knew he was coming for me."

Tom soon discovered Misty was not the pony he remembered. We don't fully understand what happened in Italy, but as Tom says: "He was in a bit of a bad state; he was stopping and going backwards. I couldn't even get him over a cross pole."

Excitement quickly turned to disappointment. Fortunately, the Whitakers had the experience to go back to basics with Misty, building his confidence and doing a couple of low key shows, jumping smaller tracks.

With Tom's determination and hard work at home the partnership seemed to gel and it wasn't long before they had some good results including two second place rosettes at Wales and West Show and over the summer good results at Hickstead and a first place at Driffield Agricultural Show in July.

In August they travelled north to the Scottish Home Pony International to compete in the HOYS Leading Pony Showjumper of the Year qualifier at Rowallan Equestrian Centre in Lanark.

At that time, Heather was in her early 20's and studying at the University of Edinburgh. She made the trip to Lanark to see her old pony and it was the first time she and Misty had seen one another since he was moved from the farm at Whithorn. Heather was sure Misty remembered her as he kept looking for the polo mints she always used to give him when her papa wasn't looking. Graeme, Heather's partner, was with her and the cheeky pony kept putting his ears back at him, while cuddling up to Heather.

Tom achieved good results at the show in Lanark including a win in one of the junior open classes. In the Leading Pony Showjumper of the Year qualifier, which was the biggest class of the show, the pair finished just outside the qualifying places. Only the top three got a

HOYS ticket so Tom was disappointed as it seemed they had just missed out.

A few weeks after the show he was notified that something had happened, perhaps one of the combinations in the line-up had already qualified and the qualifying place would go down the line to Misty and him. It was a stroke of good luck for them and they would compete at the prestigious final after all. HOYS had now moved from Wembley Arena to Birmingham NEC.

By now, Tom had learned how to get the best out of Misty. He realised the pony had to be revved up to perform at his best.

"Give him half a chance and he would do it," he says. "He was an easy pony, but if you just sat quiet he could be lazy. If you rode like you weren't bothered he'd have a pole down. The harder you rode the better he went." Tom's favourite memory is their incredible success in the Leading Pony Showjumper of the Year final at HOYS in Birmingham NEC, at the end of their season together. They went as the underdogs, as Misty was yet to prove himself as the winner he had been before going to Italy. They rode into the curtained HOYS area and went clear in the first round over the 1.40m course. A brilliant jump-off followed and the jumps went up an extra 5cm.

Pippa Allen, who was only twelve years old at the time, was first to go in the jump off and set the target in the eight strong jump off with her talented pony Spot the Lady. No one could beat her until James Smith and Mr Nice Guy took 600th of a second off their time to go into the lead. Zoe Adams and VIP Tixylix were next but couldn't beat the time leaving the jumps up. Some of the other leading pony and rider combinations in the jump off included Louise Saywell on Little Ryan, Danielle Willett on Gold Harvest, Jessie Drea on Quantum Light and Matthew Sampson on Lakeland Little Wonder. They all gave a great effort and the crowd were thrilled, but James Smith's round seemed unbeatable.

That was until Thomas rode in last to go with Miami Bound and they presented one of the finest rounds of the show, unexpectedly shaving over two seconds off James Smith's time to win, taking a turn his dad told him not to make and stunning the crowd with an unprecedented clear at a phenomenal speed. The atmosphere in the arena was ecstatic.

They had achieved what Tom's sister Ellen had hoped to do four years earlier, and won the most prestigious title in pony showjumping.

Ellen had said it was more nerve-racking watching Tom jump than competing herself, so she understood how her parents must have felt when she was riding.

Miami Bound seemed to love the spotlight and stood posing as he was presented the most prestigious title in pony show jumping. This was the fourth time he had been at HOYS and the fourth time in the presentation, his second win there. The bigger the crowd it seemed, the more he wanted to please them.

Having just won the 148cm 'championship of championships' and the biggest junior prize at HOYS, Thomas was reported as saying, when presented with the prize by his uncle John, that it was the 'fastest round of his life, it was absolutely amazing.' Photo by Anthony Reynolds LMPA

Mark McGowan was the course builder that year and remembers it like yesterday;

"Pippa Allen came into the jump-off first to set the standard and then each rider after came close, until James Smith beat their time," he says. "Tom came in last to go and nailed it. I only had two years as the course designer at HOYS, but this was one of the best finishes to a class I can remember. The crowd were packed in and they went wild!

I can remember Bob Ellis [London 2012 Olympic course designer] looking down at me from the other end of the arena and clapping his hands in recognition of my achievement. Meanwhile the tears were streaming down my face! For a pony like Miami Bound to give me the result that I hoped for as a course designer, on such a big stage, is something I will cherish for the rest of my career."

It is so nice to hear this point of view from the course designer and what the performance meant to him that day.

The *Galloway Gazette*, which was the local paper where Misty was born, featured an article about the two ponies who had taken the top two placings in HOYS biggest junior class. James Smith is based only a few miles from the Boam's farm where Misty was born in Kirkcudbrightshire.

Tom's daredevil riding style didn't always pay off. At Olympia that December, they went clear in the first round, but Thomas turned Misty too tight into a fence in the jump-off and knocked it down. "Rider error," grins Tom.

Tom rode Misty for less than eight months, but the ride had a lasting impact on him. Coming from a family who makes a living out of buying and selling horses and ponies it was unusual for Tom to have such a good pony to ride.

"Before him I'd never had such a good pony" says Tom fondly. "Misty had a big character for a little pony. The more you gave him to do the better he liked it. He got really stuck in and would turn himself inside out to jump. He was the best one I had – I always got the difficult ones no one wanted" Tom adds wryly.

Tom's success with Misty gave him a confidence boost for the future and he went on to win a Grand Prix on a horse soon after.

Misty's breeder, John, says the pony was incredibly fortunate to have been brought back to the UK by Steven. His knowledge and experience along with Tom's talent as a rider played a big part in getting him back to his best. While researching this book John asked Steven and wife Carole what they thought of the pony. For a man of few words Steven gave him high praise indeed, remembering him as a "good 'un". Carole says he was a lovely pony and has fond memories, as he was ridden by all their children: Ellen in 2001, Joe briefly at the end of 2001, Thomas in 2006 and Donald in 2008.

Tom moved onto horses full time at the end of 2006 so Miami Bound was then ridden by George Whitaker, Tom's younger cousin. George was already competing on two other 148cm ponies – Karlando and Cavalcade.

George was able to enjoy a full season competing Misty.

Now back to his old form, the pony just got better and better. They clicked straight away and won a JA Winter 148cm qualifier in February. He was, as George says: "An easy pony – very fast – one of the fastest ponies ever, you could turn him up to any fence." He also loved the fact that he was "quite bouncy and always pulling you." In the experienced hands of the Whitakers Miami Bound bloomed again.

George took Misty to compete at the Pony of the Year show at Arena UK in April and had some good placings, picking up £300 in the coveted JA Grand Prix for fifth place. Only two had made it through to the jump-off to compete for the first prize of £2,000.

In May, they won both Pony European Viewing Trials at Kenyon Equestrian Centre, on consecutive days. These trials attract all the leading pony combinations as it is part of the European team selection process, so to win both these major competitions was a remarkable achievement.

George's results with Miami Bound played a part in his selection for the John Whitaker International Squad. This programme was aimed at establishing a foundation for young riders competing successfully on the international stage. It was sponsored by John and Clare Whitaker, who are very supportive of young riders and keen to develop opportunities for them. Twelve youngsters were chosen, and teams were picked to compete for British Showjumping in the European Championships in the summer.

George was thrilled that his success had earned him a place in the Pony Nations Cup team to compete in Aach,

Germany in early June. The British team comprised of George and Miami Bound, Zoe Adams riding VIP Tixylix, Jesse Drea riding Quantum Light and Trilbie Cook riding Clogherboy Mirah.

Misty was well travelled and no doubt would have seen some of his former European equine competitors again in Germany. Pony showjumping teams took part from all around Europe, including Ireland and Italy. Each rider jumped two rounds and at the end of the competition, Great Britain came out on top. The team had worked together and pulled off some fantastic jumping, supporting each other over a very challenging course. Ireland and France finished joint second.

For the Individual Grand Prix George remembers things did not go as well. Something went wrong at a combination in the jump-off and Misty jammed the brakes on, tossing George straight through the fence.

"I don't know why he did it," George says. "He just didn't like it on that day, or maybe I was too confident? Usually if you got him there in the right place he would jump it.

"Misty got me jumping some good big pony classes and getting results – he definitely got me going."

Two weeks after the trip to Germany, they went to Pyecombe Horse Show in West Sussex where they qualified for HOYS by winning the Pony Showjumper of the Year qualifier. George was delighted Miami Bound would have a chance to defend his title at HOYS. George's older brother, William, had won the title in 2005 with Indien de Here and, of course, cousin Tom had won it in 2006 with Misty.

The Hickstead Derby meeting, also in West Sussex, was only a few days after Pyecombe. George and most of the other leading pony riders were there to try and win the Junior Masters Championship, which had a generous £2000 first prize.

Qualifiers for the Championship were held during the week and George and Misty easily made it through to the final. Unfortunately the weather was terrible so the Championship had to be moved out of Hickstead's international arena, to save the going for the famous senior DFS Derby. The Junior Masters Championship would be held in one of Hickstead's outer rings, instead.

Only eight started, due to the conditions and terrible rain, so it was decided the final would be held over one round straight against the clock. George and Miami Bound did extremely well to go clear, which was good enough for second place and £1,250 prize money. George was used to riding in all conditions at home, his hard work and commitment to training paid off on that day, as did Misty's sure-footedness and ability to perform no matter what. His first name as a foal was Storm after all.

The bigger, long striding pony Mr Bon Ami, ridden by talented young rider Pippa Allen, took the first prize of £2000 that day.

Their next show was closer to home, at the Great Yorkshire Show in July. Britain's wettest June on record presented major challenges with the ground, but George and Misty were not deterred. After jumping an impressive clear in the first round of the Junior Open Championship, they jumped clear again in the jump-off for third place.

Due to the slippery ground George didn't risk making the tight turns they could have and was delighted with the award at such a prestigious show.

Misty enjoyed an easier few weeks after achieving so many great results, which allowed him to rest up before HOYS. Meanwhile, George was working hard competing on his other ponies and had qualified Karlando for the Squibb Group Pony Foxhunter Championship, as well as the Leading Pony Showjumper of the Year final, meaning he would have two ponies to compete in the class.

At home, Misty was a constant source of amusement, keeping everyone entertained with his larger than life personality. There was a small step in the doorway of his stable, which he could get the very tips of his hooves onto and look over his doorway, appearing to anyone who didn't know him as if he were a 17hh horse. He also had his old habit of opening his door with his mouth and often went wandering around the yard, when the door hadn't been bolted securely enough.

When it was time for HOYS in October, Misty was fresh and eager to get back out jumping. Most of the Nations Cup winning team and Junior European gold medal team members would be competing in the Leading Pony Showjumper of the Year final, including European gold medal winner VIP Tixylix, ridden by Zoe Adams.

The course, which was designed by a Portuguese course designer, caused a lot of problems. Misty and George made the course look easy and they were the first to jump a clear round. The only other clear came from Jessie Drea on her pony Quantum Light. George proved his riding ability by also jumping a clear round with his other pony Karlando but unfortunately they had two time faults. This result guaranteed them third place since all the other combinations had knocked at least one jump down and occurred four faults or more.

George and Miami Bound and Jessie with Quantum Light would jump off against the clock for the title.

First to go in the jump-off, George went for it and under the instruction of his uncle Steven, pulled off some terrific turns. The crowd gasped as they turned so tight up to a 1.45m upright, turning on a sixpence. They left every fence up and crossed the finish, cheered on by older brother William and the rest of the Whitaker family. George and Miami Bound had a fast time with no faults, putting pressure on Jessie and her pony.

Jessie also navigated an incredible round and was clear until the very last fence. As Jessie went to take a stride out Quantum Light touched the pole and it fell – meaning Misty had won the most coveted title in junior show-jumping in consecutive years. He was only the second pony in the show's history to achieve such a feat. The last pony to win the title back-to-back was Kangaroo, ridden by Nicola Loffett in 1966 and 1967.

Misty does not have a huge stride, but he is brave, careful and scopey. George used that to his advantage to fulfil his childhood ambition of a lap of honour under the spotlights at HOYS. Misty again delighted in the atmosphere as he collected his third win at the prestigious show. It would be their final competition together, as Steven's youngest son, Donald, was now ready to ride him.

George Whitaker and Miami Bound winning HOYS Leading Pony Showjumper of the Year final. Miami Bound took this title in both 2006 and 2007. Photo by Steve Dawe at Real Time Imaging

After his time with Misty, who helped showcase his riding talent, George was given another five ponies to compete. George now rides horses professionally and has his own yard. He is one of Great Britain's most talented young riders, and was selected for both the British Equestrian Federation's World Class Development Programme and the Athenaeum Young Riders Academy programme, set up by the European Equestrian Federation.

Steven Whitaker's youngest son, Donald, was the fifth and final member of the Whitaker family to compete Misty after cousin George's success in 2007. Steven had secured some sponsorship with Shearwater Insurance Services and the prefix Shearwater was given to Miami Bound's British Showjumping name.

Donald gained experience jumping in the bigger classes and achieved some impressive results with Misty. They got to know each other competing at the English Home Pony International show at Southview Equestrian Centre in October 2007, just a few weeks after Misty had won at HOYS with George. In January 2008 they were fourth in the Junior Open at Arena UK.

Donald's biggest win came when they travelled to Lummen in Belgium in May 2008 and spectacularly won the Lummen Grand Prix against some of the top European competitors. There must have been some familiar rivals who Misty would have recognised from over the years. It was Donald's first competition abroad and he was delighted to have won.

After that confidence boost they hit a good run of form on their return to the UK. They jumped two brilliant clear rounds in the Leading Pony Showjumper qualifier, finishing in second place at Weston Lawns Equestrian Centre in June. This qualified them for the HOYS final again, giving Misty a chance to reclaim his title, for the third year in a row.

After they qualified for HOYS they gave Misty a few weeks off. Their next results came in August when they took home £140 for second place in the 148cm Grand Prix at Port Royal Showground. The next competition was at Southview Equestrian Centre, a week later, and they came second and fourth in two of the open classes. At Myerscough College, in September, they won the 148cm open class before the two-day show at Barton Equestrian Centre. This was their last show before HOYS, and they won and came second in two of the biggest open classes.

Misty's breeder, John, was still proudly following the talented pony's career – and he was delighted when he heard Misty would be back at HOYS, for a third year running.

"When we found out he had qualified for HOYS again we booked tickets to go and watch the final," says John. "We hadn't been able to go to watch in previous years, but we didn't want to miss the chance again."

"Katie, Joan and I managed to get tickets to watch him in the warm-up arena as well as in the class. It was great to see him after hearing about all his amazing results over the years."

Donald Whitaker and Miami Bound competing at HOYS in the Leading Pony Showjumper of the Year final 2008. Photo by Steve Dawe at Real Time Imaging

Donald and Misty were 25th to go out of 26 in the class and the course was causing a lot of faults. Even for the experienced ponies, including Misty, it was not meant to be and they finished their round with an unfortunate pole down. There were only four clears through to the jump-off and the eventual winner was Roberta Roe on an old rival New York Spritzer. It was the first time the pony had won the class, but it was well deserved. Like Miami Bound, New York Spritzer had been there several times with different riders and was placed seventh back in 2001 with Louise Pavitt, at the time when Miami Bound was second with Ellen Whitaker.

Showjumping isn't a science and success is never guaranteed, because so many factors can play a part in the performance on the day. It is always great to see fellow competitors support each other and celebrate success, even if things don't go their way on the day. Showjumpers, especially the junior riders, are very good at that.

The year 2008 was the last year Miami Bound would compete at HOYS, a show he had won three titles at, as well as being placed there three times. Donald was disappointed he didn't get to finish on a high, but qualifying itself is a great achievement and it was a good experience to compete in 'the biggest pony class in the world'. Donald was destined to go onto horses, and so it was also their last competition together.

Towards the end of 2008 Jessica Crosby started competing on Misty for owner, Steven. Jessica's family own a riding school and equestrian centre nearby and are good friends with the Whitakers. Jessica was a competitive and talented youngster and seemed to click straight away with the super grey pony.

By sheer coincidence, Jessica had also started competing on the pony Mr Nice Guy, who was runner up to Miami Bound in the 2006 Leading Pony Showjumper of the Year Championship at HOYS. James Smith and Mr Nice Guy were also runner up in the same final in 2008. The two former rivals had become stable mates!

Misty and Jessica won their first class together, a Junior Open at Port Royal Equestrian Centre in November 2008. This was a venue they seemed to do well at and had five wins there during their eleven months together.

Morc good rcsults followcd, at most of the major UK premier junior shows including Ingliston Equestrian Centre in February 2009 where they qualified for the Winter JA Classic final, to be held in the summer at The Royal Show. Jessica would also qualify Mr Nice Guy for the same final.

They had a first place again at the Wales and West Show in May, taking home the £150 first prize in the 148 Grand Prix. Next was the South View Equestrian Centre's Summer European Viewing trials. At that time, Katie was helping out at the show in the sponsors tent and managed to watch Misty jump. She got to have a chat with Jessica and her dad and watch Miami Bound compete in one of the classes. They had a win in the 1.15m open out of a large field and contested the pony European viewing trials, which were around 1.30m.

Jessica Crosby and Miami Bound at the Scope Festival of Showjumping 2009. Image from Graham Loader, Thefotographer.

Their last competition together was the BSJA/Scope Festival of Showjumping in September at Staffordshire showground, where they won one of the 148cm open classes.

It was decided Steven would sell Misty after Jessica had finished the 2009 season. When a viewing was arranged, Misty went to John Whitaker's yard, so that George, who was based with John at the time, could ride him.

Norway Bound

Miami Bound was sold to Norway at the end of 2009

It was the Ulven family from Oslo, Norway who had arranged to view Miami Bound. They had got to know about him through a Swedish man called Fredrik Jansson, who knew the Whitakers. Per Ulven was looking for a pony to compete in bigger pony showjumping competitions and his sister, Lisa, was also interested in the sport. The family travelled over to England to see him at John Whitaker's yard and George rode him to show them what he could do.

"Of course we could see immediately what a super pony he was and we liked him at once," says Lena, Per and Lisa's mother. "Per thought he was easy to ride and it was an instant match between them."

Miami Bound left the Whitaker's yard and joined the Ulven family in Norway. They already had four other ponies, who had come from England, so he was in good company. It is usual that horses and ponies are called the first name on their passport, so Miami Bound was known in the stable as 'Miami'.

Per won a bronze medal with him in the Norwegian championships the following year and, as Lena says, "he won most of the classes he started". They travelled to some major pony competitions including Odense in

Denmark, Hengelo in the Netherlands, as well Drammen in Norway.

In one of the last competitions Per rode him in, they won the jump off by six seconds, even though Per took a wrong turn and lost a second or two. "Isn't that amazing? He was still so quick on the course," says Lena.

When Lisa 'inherited' Miami from her brother, she initially struggled a bit with him, until she learned to ride a little more forcefully. Lena remembers his mischief with great affection.

"He really has a lot of character, he always untied himself and if he got bored he bent his head down and nuzzled me in my stomach!" she says. "I remember once we were queuing for a while in a trot-up line in Drammen in Norway and he got really bored and nearly pushed me over with his nuzzling antics, but it was difficult to be angry with him."

Another of his tricks, that was not so popular, was his habit of untying himself.

"For sure he likes mud," recalls Lena. "He drove Lisa crazy sometimes, especially at shows when she had showered him and tied him up in the stable. Yes you can imagine what happened! But apart from that he really is a lovely pony."

Katie found contact details for Lena after researching details via the Norwegian Equestrian Federation in 2011.

"I asked Carole Whitaker about him and she had told us he was now in Norway," says Katie. "We just wanted to see how he was getting on and it was really kind that Lena was happy to hear from us and send pictures."

During the winter months, Miami and the Ulven's other ponies returned to England to the yard of their trainer, Norwegian showjumper, Morten Aasen.

"The winters in Norway can reach -20 degrees," Lena says. "All our ponies stayed in England at Morten's yard during December and January where the winters were warmer. It was good for the ponies and also for us, having some time off. Miami went with our other ponies – Edsillia, Cevin III, Corrib and Sandilands Milton Merlin – most of whom had been purchased from well-known English riders. The ponies had a good friendship and travelled a lot together."

While Miami was at Morten Aasen's yard in England, Katie arranged to visit him on 2 January 2012, along with her husband Ade and their eighteen-month-old daughter, Grace.

"It was really nice to see him looking so well and enjoying time out in the field," recalls Katie. "It was a sunny day and we spent some time feeding him carrots and taking pictures. Grace loved him straight away and he seemed happy to see us.

"All the ponies had rugs on out in the field, except for Misty. The groom was a little irritated as he kept taking his rug off, but I had to laugh. His antics hadn't changed!" recalls Katie.

Lena was planning to visit the ponies the following weekend, because Lisa needed to start riding them again in preparation for the Sunshine Tour in Spain. The ponies were going directly from England to Spain in February, travelling in a very large and comfortable horsebox.

Lisa had a lot of success on the Spanish Sunshine Tour, which is also very popular with British riders and their young horses. It allows the horse and rider to gain experience competing before the start of the showjumping season in the UK, or indeed Norway. Lisa and her ponies had 11 first places and a lot of seconds and thirds, winning most of these on Miami in 1.10m and 1.20m classes.

His jumping prowess over the years made Miami quite a legend in the showjumping circles, and many show-jumpers on the Tour remembered him.

"He is still a star and almost everyone recognised him and wanted to say hello," Lisa remembers fondly. "Miami was a superstar down there and a lot of people came to have a look at the famous English pony."

Lena appreciated Miami and the experiences he gave Per and Lisa. "Miami is a fantastic pony with a great personality. My children have had great success with him during the time we have had him. Unfortunately, they got too tall for him and needed to move on to horses."

Since moving on to horses, Per and Lisa have become amongst Norway's leading young riders and Lisa still competes successfully in Grand Prix classes all around Europe.

Lisa Ulven and Miami Bound had much success at the Spanish Sunshine Tour in the spring of 2012.

Best of Friends

Miami Bound left a lasting impression on Nora Larsen Nalbant; 'He was an amazing teacher of a pony for me' recalls Nora.

Nora was just eleven years old when her parents decided she could have her own pony.

Nora regularly had lessons at the same stables where the Ulven family kept Miami and her trainer recommended him as a good first pony. She had seen Miami many times; "he was an incredible, beautiful pony," says Nora "I remember my friends getting very jealous when they heard I was going to ride him. They all had seen the video on YouTube of George Whitaker winning a big class at the Horse of the Year Show and they knew how good he was. I didn't want to buy him at first, because I thought of him as a pony that was way too good and too difficult for me to ride."

But her trainer's instinct for the pony was right and Nora soon discovered he was a gentle, calm pony who was not complicated to ride. She became nervous though when her trainer put up a fence for her to jump.

"I was a little bit scared because I had not jumped a lot before," says Nora. "But Miami was a star, as he always is, and jumped the fence without any problem at all. He made my nerves go away and at that point I knew Miami and I would be the perfect fit."

The more Nora rode Miami, the more her confidence grew. Within six months she went from a novice jumper to competing in 1m classes.

Nora loved the beauty of Miami and his gentle ability to teach her to ride, what she liked best about him was his bravery. Miami wasn't afraid of anything and even when all the other ponies around him were spooking, he took it all in his stride.

"Miami would just stand there and watch their antics, clearly wondering why they even bothered getting so crazy," Nora says. "I could not have asked for a better first pony than him, because he was so safe."

Nora has many happy memories about her time with Miami Bound, "I enjoyed everything about my time with Miami. The late evenings preparing him for a show the following day, the times we competed, all the hours I spent in the stable with him, and so much more. I share so many beautiful memories with him."

A favourite memory is competing in a 1m speed class together for the first time. "I planned how to ride the course along with my trainer," Nora recalls. "At one place in the course you could choose between making a short turn or a wide turn, from one fence to another. My trainer told me to make the wide one, but I knew Miami and me would be able to do the short one".

"I went in the ring and Miami jumped the course perfectly. Despite my trainer's advice, I made the short turn, which Miami handled easily. We won the class with good margins and I remember being very happy and proud to have this pony."

Nora came to know everything about Miami's habits. "Each time he was back in his stable after being ridden, the first thing he did was to lie down and roll not one, but two times."

She fondly remembers all of his quirks. The funny low noise he makes sometimes with his mouth and the way he would do a little jump in the air if she touched his back with her hand if she was riding him. How every time she groomed him, and then walked out of his sight to get something, he would start scraping on the floor

Miami Bound gave his young rider Nora great confidence jumping

with a hoof and refuse to stop until she came back. Then there was the way he would start scratching her back when she scratched his shoulder, as if to say, "thank you."

While Nora was competing at a show in May 2013, Miami tripped on landing over the last jump in the course and stumbled. Fortunately Nora wasn't badly hurt after the fall, but Miami damaged his tendon. He was sent back to the UK for specialist treatment from the vets at Morten Aasen's yard in England. Luckily, after treatment and rest the injury healed perfectly and he was able to return to work. Miami went back to Norway in May 2014 when it was decided he could go on to teach another young rider.

When the time came to say goodbye to Miami, Nora was both sad and happy. She was sad because she had to say goodbye to the pony that meant so much to her, as he had taught her so much and made her the rider she is today. But, with a maturity beyond her years, Nora was also happy.

As she says "I knew another rider would get the same opportunity as I had. The opportunity to be taught by this amazing teacher of a pony."

A Schoolmaster

It was Marianne Sundal who found Miami Bound for his next rider, Elin Martine Mehren.

Marianne is the owner of a riding school and livery yard in Lier, Norway. Elin Martine lives next door to the stables and had become good friends with Fanny, Marianne's daughter. It was Fanny who introduced Elin Martine to all the ponies, and the two girls took riding lessons together.

Elin Martine started riding at the age of seven and her trainer, Marianne, had a big impact and influence on her equestrian achievements. As well as her riding skills, Marianne taught Elin Martine how to care for and handle horses and ponies.

When Elin Martine was eight years old she asked her parents when she would be able to have a pony of her own. They told her she would have to wait until she was twelve years old. Like most parents, they thought by that time the desire would have worn off.

In April 2014, the month before Elin Martine's twelve birthday, Marianne told her parents she would learn a great deal if it were possible she could have her own pony. If her parents were willing, she would find something suitable. After a few days mulling Marianne's words over, Elin Martine's parents finally agreed.

After a few days of searching Marianne found Miami Bound, a pony who was now in his twenties. Marianne got in touch with the owners who told them he had been in England for a year with a tendon injury. However, the injury had fully repaired and he was ready to start work again.

Miami Bound duly arrived, in great secrecy, Elin Martine did not know anything about him. Marianne asked her if she would like to try a pony she was considering for the riding school, not letting on that the pony was actually for her. Elin Martine replied: "Of course. Yes."

When the two met, the first thing the still mischievous Miami Bound did was to take Elin Martine's cap off her head, which greatly amused her. She laughed and gave him a big hug, liking the pony immediately, but still having no clue that he was for her.

Miami was led into the indoor school and she got on, trotted around and did some small jumps. Marianne was delighted at how well the two were suited. Elin Martine's mother, Ragnhild, says she will "never forget her face when we asked if she'd like to have him as her own."

Elin Martine also remembers the day well. "It was May 18th 2014. He had a good personality and was excellent to jump. And he had birthday on the same day as me – June 26th!"

Elin Martine took great care of Miami. She gave him supplements and looked after his feet. She took him on long hacks, strengthening his muscles and he became a strong, good looking Miami, thriving on the love and attention and delighting everyone with his mischievous antics.

Elin Martine worked hard to get Miami Bound back to fitness and the pair went on to win the Winter Cup competition in April 2015.

“He loved it when Elin Martine played with him,” says Ragnhild. “He was the stable imp. After each competition, she went for a long walk with him and cooled down his legs. And every evening he got some carrots, which he loved.”.

The two got on very well and Elin Martine enjoyed each competition they did together, usually finishing in the top three places. One of Elin Martine’s favourite competitions was winning the Winter Cup 90cm Showjumping competition. She learned a lot from Miami’s care and experience.

“He taught me to jump and to control my nerves and that he was to be trusted,” she says. “He is one in a million and I loved him very much.”

Even in his twenties Miami was still as naughty as ever. He would take off his protective boots and his lips were so supple he could even pull up the zipper of Elin Martine’s jacket. He would rub his head on her and one annoying thing was that he loved to roll in the mud, so he often became brown instead of white.

A game they enjoyed playing in the indoor arena was tag, where he ran around after her and then she ran around after him.

“It was beautiful to watch a video of them playing tag together like this, similar to the game Debbie had played with him as a foal,” says Katie.

Miami had two friends on the yard: Madam, a small grey pony, and Rascal who was also called Miami Junior. Miami and Madam were best friends, even though he would often nip her bottom. Elin Martine has such fond memories of her time with him.

"Miami loved to go on tour and gallop around the fields," she says. "He had always to go first. He refused to walk, trot or gallop behind the other ponies. And he had always his ears forward, except when there was food around!"

Elin Martine loved the pony who taught her so much, as she says of their time together, "I could not have been luckier because he was so fun and taught me a lot. He helped me to many victories. As long as I dared to sit and ride him, he did everything to get a place on the podium. He did everything for me, shuffled his legs when we got a bit of an error coming towards the fence and still jumped. He loved being in the victory lap. He was the best mentor one could imagine."

It was a tough decision to retire Miami Bound, but Elin Martine was ready to jump bigger tracks, which she felt Miami Bound should not been jumping at his age.

"It was hard for him to compete at the level I was then," Elin Martine recalls sadly, "He managed one day, but not two days. We also knew he had suffered an injury in one of the legs when we bought him. It became hard for him to jump and we did not know how many times his legs had been treated. We felt very sorry for him, because he looked so sad when he couldn't manage to do his job."

"We decided he deserved a retirement, where he could live the rest of his life being taken care of and loved".

Ragnhild had been in contact with Lena Ulven, who had stayed intouch with how Miami had been getting on with his new family. Lena had mentioned to Ragnhild that it would be nice for him to retire back with his breeders, once Elin Martine was ready for a bigger horse.

It was heart-warming that Gypsy was teaching Grace to ride, since she had given both Debbie and Katie a passion for showjumping, so many years ago.

At that time, Katie was introducing her five year old daughter, Grace, to lead rein classes with Miami Bound's mum Gypsy, who was now in her 30s. Grace was proving to be pony mad, loving all aspects of looking after Gypsy.

On 4 August Katie received an email from Ragnhild about having Miami Bound back for retirement.

"Considering Gypsy is like a family member it was quite overwhelming to think we would reunite her with her first born, and offer them both a well-deserved retirement together" says Katie. "There were tears of joy and excitement all around. I'll never forget telling my Dad, who never usually shows emotion, but his eyes welled up. Miami Bound has brought a lot of joy to our family. Heather and Hugh were also delighted that they would get the chance to see him again after all these years."

Katie and Ragnhild began to put into place all that was needed for his return, a lot of paperwork and customs documents had to be sorted. He arrived at the farm in Scotland on a pleasant Saturday afternoon, on the 22 August 2015. A well-seasoned traveller, Miami, was very relaxed during the four-day journey from Norway to Scotland.

John's wife, Joan, recalls the day he returned to the family farm.

"We could do nothing less than put out the red carpet for Miami as he walked relaxed into his stable at home," she says. "It's how we felt the day he arrived. The first thing he did as he walked around in the deeply bedded stable was to have a good old roll or two, then a shake.

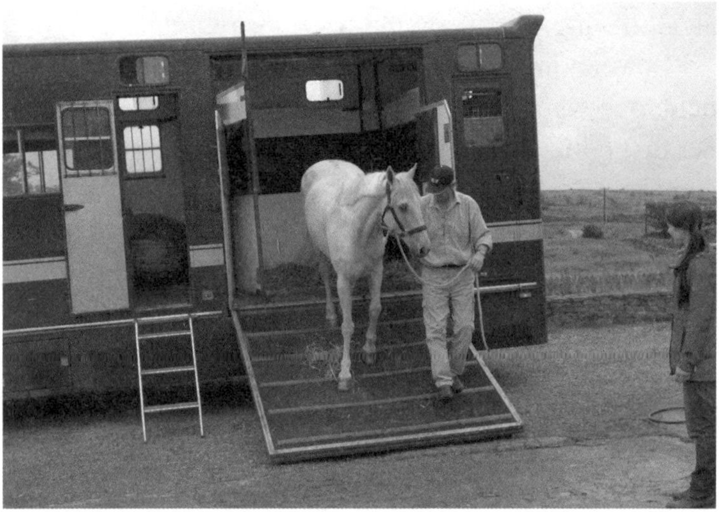

Miami Bound arrives back to the farm via Roland Holmes horse transport. Roland had helped to arrange his journey and made it as smooth as possible.

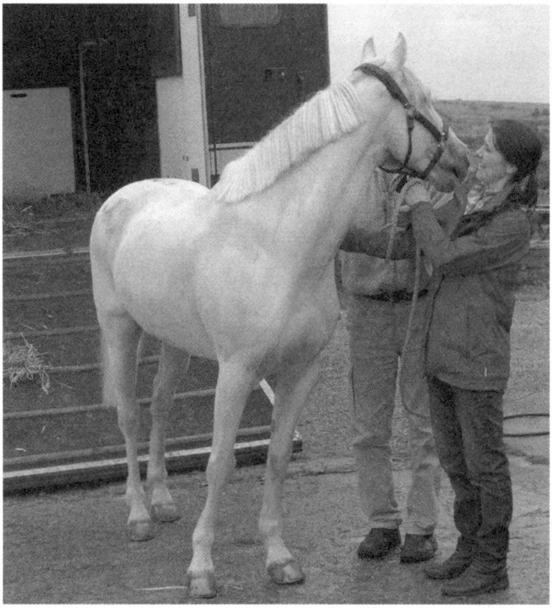

Katie thankful for Miami Bound's safe arrival from Norway.

Having a roll in his stable after a long journey

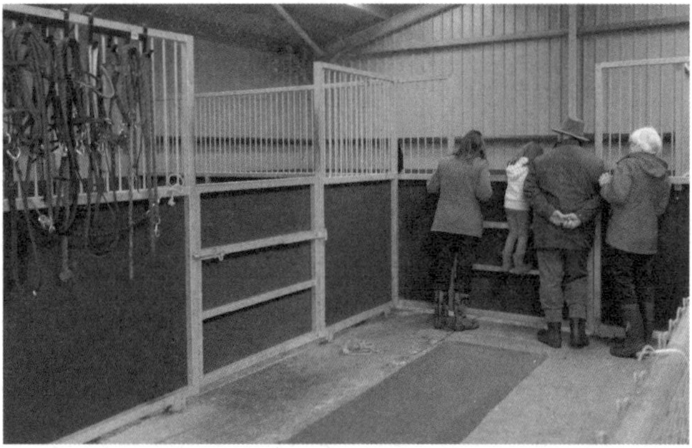

Debbie, Grace, John and Joan watching Miami have a good roll in his stable after returning home. Note the red carpet leading up to his stable!

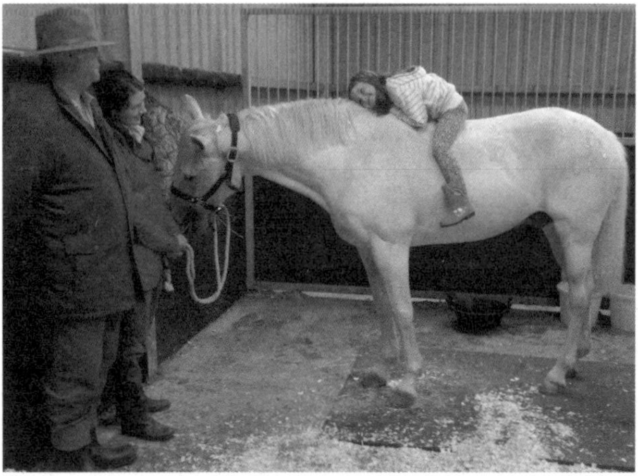

"As he stood and looked at all the eyes watching him, I wondered what his thoughts were. Ours were one of incredible excitement and happiness. 'Is he really back home?' we thought."

Joan reflected back many years, to that dappled grey, handsome little three-year-old pony, who was about to be sold, and remembered how he looked. He stood in his stable with his ears pricked, looking so bright and intelligent and unaware he was about to leave the farm.

"I wondered what the future would hold for him and hoped beyond all hopes that he would have a kind owner and be well looked after and loved," she says. "Never in our wildest dreams could we have imagined the amazing life he has had and that he would return back here one day. It is a real blessing."

Miami Bound will live out the rest of his days surrounded by the love and attention this amazing pony truly deserves, with his mother, Gypsy, often grazing in the same field he was born. He is so knowing and such a gentleman, but still has all his cheeky traits like opening his door and doing nearly anything for a Polo mint or carrot.

Grace and Misty have been to the Machars Riding Club, the same local show he started his career with Heather all of those years ago, and lots of Heather's friends who knew Miami Bound as a youngster are always pleased to see him.

Although retired, he is ridden at home by Katie and her daughter Grace. He enjoys trips to the beach and has also taken part in a local charity ride ridden by brave young showjumper, Lucy Badham, who has helped raise thousands of pounds for cancer charities during her treatment.

Grace riding Miami Bound being led by Heather at Carty Port, where the Machars Riding Club often hold competitions.

“With Gypsy now 33 years old, we are sure Miami Bound will have much more of his story to tell, teaching younger members of our family the fun of riding and doing just as much or as little as he likes,” says Katie. “We are letting him decide and thoroughly enjoying having him around”.

Back row left to right: Debbie, John, Joan, Katie. Front row left to right: Debbie’s son Lewis and Katie’s children Henry and Grace. Taken just before Miami Bound arrived back to the farm.

Grace putting the bridle on

Time out in the field, Gypsy and Miami
with Henry and Grace

Enjoying a canter along the beach,
within walking distance from the farm

List of major achievements

1995 – 1998 Heather Vance, Scotland

Heather started Miami Bound's showjumping career when she was 11 years old and Miami Bound was four. Together they went on to win numerous trophies at local unaffiliated competitions in the Machars Riding Club and Wigtown and Stranraer Agricultural Shows.

1999 – 2000 Lauley Squibb, England

1999

Three 1sts and one 2nd place in the Blue Chip Junior Newcomers first rounds

1st JC/JD Final at the Pony of the Year Show

Three 1sts and one 2nd place in the Squibb & Davies Junior Foxhunter first round

3rd Pony Newcomer Masters at the Festival Of Showjumping

1st Winter JC First Round Forest Edge Show

2000

1st Junior Open at the Pony of the Year show £100 prize

2nd Junior Open at Scope Festival of Showjumping £200 prize

1st Squibb & Davies Junior Foxhunter Masters at the Festival of Showjumping

8th Horse of the Year Show (HOYS) Squibb & Davies Junior Foxhunter Championship

1st HOYS Blue Chip Junior Newcomers Championship

2001 Ellen Whitaker, England

1st Junior Open at Wales And West Show £100 prize

1st in CSIP A4 and A7 Le Toupuet, France, as part of the Accenture Junior International Squad

1st Pony Showjumper Of The Year qualifier at Devon County

1st and two 2nd places in 148 cm Junior Open classes at the Hickstead Derby Meeting

1st Scope Promotions Festival of Showjumping £1000 148cm JA Championship

1st Grade JA at the Arena UK Festival Of Showjumping £100 prize

2nd HOYS Paul Fabrications Leading Pony Showjumper of the Year Championship (1.45m)

1st Grade JA at South View Equestrian Centre £200 prize

2002-2003 Nicola FitzGibbon, Ireland

1st RDS Dublin Horse Show (1.35m)

1st Irish Showjumping National 148cm Championship 2002 (1.35m)

1st Irish Showjumping National 148cm Speed Championship

1st Cavan Equestrian Centre two fence challenge (1.70m)

1st 6 fence challenge (1.65m)

1st Puissance (1.75m)

1st Fontainebleau Grand Prix (1.30m)

1st Diest Grand Prix
1st Team Trials Mullingar
1st Freudenberg Irish Nations Cup team
1st Irish Showjumping National 148cm Championship 2003
1st Mill Street Pony Owners Grand Prix
1st Portlaoise Grand Prix, Ireland

2004-2005 Orsola Baggio, Italy

Miami Bound's passport has fourteen FEI (International Equestrian Federation) stamps from his time in Italy. Most are from prestigious equestrian centres around Italy, but he also has one from Austria, one from Belgium and two stamps from Fontainebleau France. Miami Bound was a member of the Italian Pony Showjumping team at the European Championships. His best individual results seem to have been in Belgium (CSIO Poney de Moorsele) and France (Fontainebleau).

2006 Thomas Whitaker, England

1st Junior Open Scottish Home Pony International
1st HOYS Leading Pony Showjumper of the year
2nd Stainsby Grange Junior Open £100 prize

2007 George Whitaker, England

5th JA Grand Prix at the Pony of the Year Show £300 prize
1st Pony European Viewing Trials at Kenyon Equestrian Centre £150 prize (day 1)
1st Pony European Viewing Trials at Kenyon Equestrian Centre £150 prize (day 2)

1st GB Pony Nations Cup team at Aach, Germany.

2nd 148cm Masters Championship Hickstead £1,250 prize.

1st HOYS Leading Pony Showjumper of the year (Championship)

2008 Donald Whitaker, England

1st Lummen, Belgium Grand Prix

2nd Leading Pony Showjumper qualifier at Weston Lawns Equestrian Centre £100 prize

2nd 148cm Grand Prix at Port Royal Showground £140 prize

1st 148cm Open at Myerscough College

2nd 148cm Open at Barton Equestrian Centre £100 prize

2009 Jessica Crosby, England

Five 1sts in Junior Open classes at Port Royal Show Ground

1st Pony Members Cup Qualifier at Willerby Hill Farm

1st 148cm Open Wales and West £150 prize

1st Junior Open BSJA/Scope Festival of Showjumping

2010 – 2012 Per Ulven and Lisa Ulven, Norway

Per Ulven won a bronze medal at the Norwegian National Championships and had numerous wins and placings at major pony competitions including Odense in Denmark, Hengelo in the Netherlands and Drammen in Norway.

Lisa Ulven competed Miami Bound with success and travelled to the Spanish Sunshine tour in the spring 2012 where they won many of the 1.10m and 1.20m classes.

2012-2013 Nora Larsen Nalbant , Norway

Nora's trainer recommended Miami as a good first pony for her. Nora formed a special bond with Miami and he taught her all about jumping. The two competed successfully in showjumping competitions until Miami had an injury in May 2013.

2014- 2015 Elin Martine Mehren, Norway

Miami was Elin Martine's first pony. Elin Martine built Miami back up to fitness after his tendon injury in 2013. Together they competed successfully in showjumping, winning the 90cm Winter Cup and also competed in dressage competitions.

Prize winnings

It's difficult to put a figure on Miami Bound's total prize winnings since more than half of his competitive career was outside the UK. The FEI only started recording winnings from 2013 so there are no records for his winnings outside of the UK or Ireland. In seven years under British Showjumping registration his prize money was £10,483 (10,319 points). In two years registered with Irish SJ he accumulated 358 points in two years.

Miami Stud

A background on Miami Stud and Hugh Paterson

John, Debbie and Katie visiting Hugh's farm. Hugh in the picture with one of his other youngsters.

Hugh Peterson has built up an impressive reputation with the Scottish Sport Horse studbook (SSH) with his Miami ponies over the years. He continued to breed sport horses and ponies after his granddaughter, Heather, finished riding Misty, or Miami Mystique, as he was known then.

The first Miami pony was named back in the 1980's. John Dunlop, who was Hugh's business partner at the time, used to name his ponies after television shows. It was this that sprung to mind when Hugh was asked to name a pony he was entering for a competition. He started to say 'Miami Vice', after the television show he had seen recently, but quickly realised 'Vice' might not be a good name for a pony and swapped it for 'Maestro'. From that day on, all his ponies had the prefix 'Miami'.

Hugh's horses and ponies have taken numerous titles in the SSH loose jumping championships and many have progressed to compete in national competitions.

Miami Minstrel was bought from his local Wigtown horse and pony sales in the late 1980s, and went on to compete successfully in showjumping. Shona Mitchell was placed in the Junior Newcomers final at Horse of the Year show with the pony in 1989, narrowly missing out on a win after having one pole down in the jump-off.

In 2009 Hugh won the Central Breeders Prefix Award for his life-time contribution to breeding in recognition of the Miami name. Hugh also won the North of the Border Foal Show Championship in 2007 and 2008 and was runner up in 2009.

The aptly named Miami Gold won a European gold medal for the British pony eventing team in Italy, 2005. Miami Gold was out of a daughter of Chippie (Heather's first pony) and sired by the stallion Hocki, who Hugh and John Dunlop bought at Ballinsloe fair in Ireland as a foal.

The grey stallion Hocki was a talented showjumper.

As a six-year-old he was runner up in the Squibb and Davis Pony Foxhunter final at HOYS in 2001 with Karl Bowman. That was the same year Miami Bound was runner-up in the Leading Pony Showjumper of the Year, ridden by Ellen Whitaker.

Miami Carwyn was bred by Hugh Paterson, sired by the successful jumping pony stallion Machno Carwyn. In 2015 Miami Carwyn competed at HOYS in the Blue Chip Pony Newcomers final with Maia Andrews. It is an incredible achievement just to qualify for these finals, so it makes everyone connected incredibly proud.

Another descendant of Chippie is Miami Sandyman. He was fifth in the Squibb Group Pony Foxhunter final at HOYS in 2016, ridden by Alana Hood.

Miami Bound's full sister, Miracle bred foals for John Dunlop and they were mostly sold locally as Pony Club and competition ponies. Hugh bought one of the mares to breed with and called her Miami Moondust.

At that time, he had bred a young colt by the stallion Balougran Z with one of his pony mares. The colt was named Miami Hullabaloo and Hugh used Hullabaloo as a stallion to cover Moondust. The eventual result was a colt foal named Miami Moonbeam.

Miami Moonbeam was ridden by Nicole Kershaw and placed fifth in the Blue Chip Pony Newcomers final at HOYS in 2015, and was runner up in the Squibb Group Pony Foxhunter final in 2016. Moonbeam was purchased from Hugh by Alan Fazakerley in 2014, who hoped history would repeat itself. Miami Moonbeam was the highest placed British bred pony in this prestigious final in 2016 and for Hugh to have bred two ponies in the top five is a commendable achievement.

"It has been interesting to watch the success of ponies bred by Hugh and see the descendants of Miracle, carrying on Gypsy's bloodline, and Chippie do so well over the years" says Katie. "In 2015 and 2016 several connections to the ponies travelled down from Scotland to support them at HOYS; Heather, Julie (who lives near Hugh and is a help with all the youngsters), Beth McDonald (who first started competing Miami Moonbeam) and myself with daughter, Grace. Hugh was eagerly awaiting news from his home, unable to make the long journey but we all cheered them on after their rounds, it was a great experience especially since they did so well."

There have been many other talented Miami ponies and recently Hugh started using the prefix on his horses. One of the most successful horses he bred was Cree Cruiser, who came second in the Puissance final at HOYS in 2009 and jumped in four senior Nations Cup teams for Great Britain. Heather is now riding his young horses, a bay stallion called Miami Boy Cruiser and a young mare by him called Miami Voltaira.

Hugh is now in his 80s and still likes to do as much as he can. One of the pony foals he has at the moment is Miami Gold Sands, who has every bloodline from all of his years of breeding, including Chippie and Moondust.

Talking to Hugh about his memories has often brought a lump to his throat, he is incredibly proud of what his

Miami horses and ponies have achieved over the years. He gets a lot of pleasure watching Heather ride and continues to instruct her from the sidelines, always encouraging her to jump higher. Hugh is a true character and despite his lifetime experience with horses, he says, "you never stop learning".

Heather with Misty and her papa Hugh, of Miami Stud.

Pride and Joy Farm

A little more about Gypsy and her legacy

Gypsy and Tinker

After Katie's younger brother Luke had grown too tall for riding Gypsy, it was decided to try her for another foal. This proved difficult, so she was sent to a local stud with a specialist equine reproductive veterinarian. The resident stallion was a well-bred ex-racehorse called Vitus, sired by the successful Thoroughbred Dancing Brave. Vitus had been in training with Sir Henry Cecil and had been lightly raced, but had an almost fatal injury. Gypsy came back home in foal to Vitus. Eleven months later the family took turns to watch Gypsy during the night in case she had any difficulties foaling. "I remember her foaling very well, at 5.30am, it was Dad's shift and he woke everyone up to watch the birth of a beautiful bay filly. We called her Tinker" recalls Katie

Tinker did everything from hacking out, beach rides and local shows, even Mum and Debbie rode her. Tinker bred two foals – Taylor and Belle – and both were nice projects to bring on and sell as riding ponies.

Hugh had Gypsy at Miami Stud for a summer, once Tinker was weaned, to run with his young colt Miami Hullabalou.

Gypsy was scanned at the end of the season, but wasn't in foal. She stayed for a few weeks longer before coming back to the farm. Miraculously, the following summer, Gypsy was showing in foal and had a coloured colt in August who Luke named Apache. In 2016 Apache had a good season jumping affiliated, with a talented young Scottish rider Lucy Bainbridge-Craig. Apache is Gypsy's last foal (born in 2008) sired by Miami Stud's stallion Miami Hullabalou.

Tinker was sold locally in 2016 to Heather Vance's cousin, Jenni Brooke, who is doing all sorts of activities with the Galloway Pony Club.

Miracle, who was a full sister to Miami Bound, suffered an injury from another horse while at the Dunlop's farm and unfortunately had to be put down in 2014. On finding this out, Katie bought Miracle's last daughter, a grey mare sired by Hocki, and called her Angel.

Angel is now at the family farm, which Katie calls

‘Pride and Joy Farm’ with a daughter of Apache called Geronimo, these two fillies will continue Gypsy’s bloodline. It is surprising how similar in attitude Gypsy’s offspring have been, rather independent and full of character. It is a real pleasure to see them thrive and exciting to look to the future and wonder what stories will unfold for them. If they produce half as much talent as their ‘uncle’ Miami Bound, we will be delighted.

Misty and Tinker grazing together, most of the ponies at 'Pride and Joy farm' are descendants of Gypsy.

Miami Bound's nieces Angel and Mo, both in foal for 2017

Storm as a foal with his dark grey coat

Storm as a 2 year old

Lady (on the left) and Storm as youngsters at the Boam family's farm

Picture of Lady and Storm at the back, a lovely picture with a rainbow over them.

Debbie with Storm age 3 years old (on the left) and Lady aged 2 years old.

Heather introduced Misty to all the local competitions.

Heather and Misty became an inseparable partnership during his younger years.

Heather with Misty and Katie with Gypsy meeting up at a local show, the ponies recognised each other with a gentle whinny.

Heather and Misty went on to win many local trophies together until Heather grew too tall for him.

Lauley Squibb and Miami Bound. Blue Chip Junior Newcomers Champions at the Horse of the Year Show.

Horse of the Year Show Champions Lauley Squibb and Miami Bound.
Photo by Anthony Reynolds LMPA

Ellen Whitaker with Miami Bound en route to a terrific Dunglenn 148cm Championship victory at Scope Festival of Showjumping 2001

Nicola FitzGibbon and Miami Bound RHS Dublin Horse Show 148cm winner. Photo by Tony Parkes Photographer

Having just won the 148cm 'championship of championships' and the biggest junior prize at HOYS, Thomas was reported as saying, when presented with the prize by his uncle John, that it was the 'fastest round of his life, it was absolutely amazing.' Photo by Anthony Reynolds LMPA

Miami Bound Jumping 1.45m at the Horse of the Year Show with Thomas Whitaker as they won the Leading Junior Showjumper of the Year final in 2006.

George Whitaker and Miami Bound winning HOYS Leading Pony Showjumper of the Year final. Miami Bound took this title in both 2006 and 2007. Photo by Steve Dawe at Real Time Imaging

Donald Whitaker and Miami Bound competing at HOYS in the Leading Pony Showjumper of the Year final 2008.
Photo by Steve Dawe at Real Time Imaging

Jessica Crosby and Miami Bound at the Scope Festival of Showjumping 2009. Image from Graham Loader, Thefotographer.

Lisa Ulven and Miami Bound had much success at the Spanish Sunshine Tour in the spring of 2012.

Katie visited Misty in January 2012, “Misty seemed very interested in Grace, little did we know then that she would get the chance to ride him when she was older” says Katie.

Nora was just eleven years old when her parents decided she could have her own pony; Miami Bound.

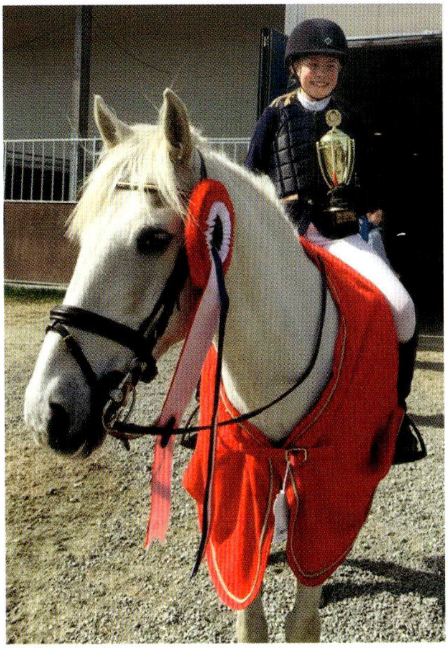

Winners of the Winter Cup
competition April 2015

Elin Martine and Miami Bound
celebrating on 17 May, the annual
Norwegian constitution day.

Elin Martine enjoyed riding Miami and
they formed a special partnership

The winter in Norway was
very cold with a lot of snow!

Elin Martine loved Miami Bound very much, saying goodbye to him was difficult once she was ready to ride a bigger horse.

Miami Bound arriving back at the farm where he was born for his retirement in August 2015.

Enjoying time out in the field, relaxing, rolling and having a play.

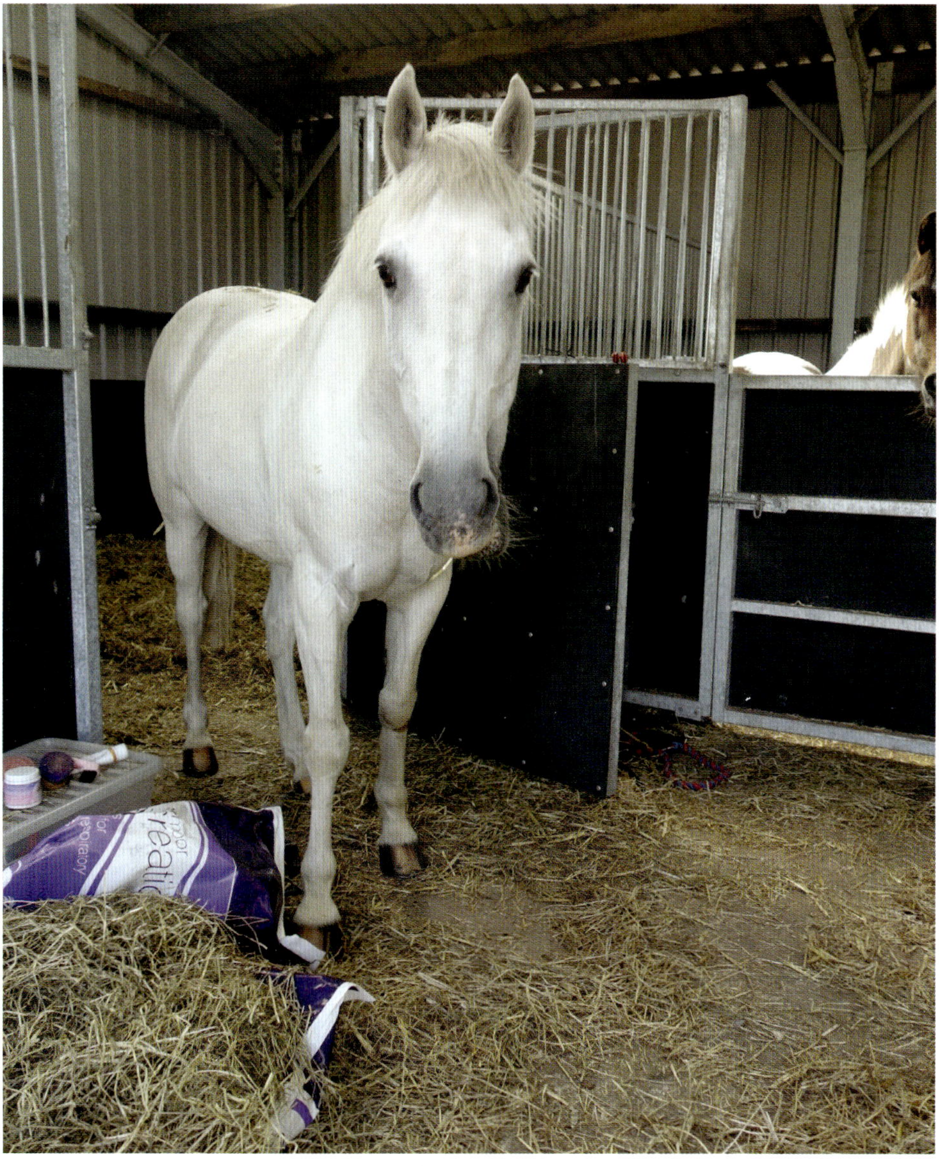

Still up to his old antics of opening the stable door

Grace riding Miami Bound being led by Heather at Carty Port, where the Machars Riding Club often hold competitions.

Riding out on the beach, ears pricked enjoying watching the sea gulls and having a splash in the sea.

Ears pricked enjoying hacking around the farm tracks, what a beautiful view!

Grace and Misty forming a bond, he is so gentle with young ones.

Lazy days out in the field with Gypsy, Misty's mum

Heather and Misty January 2017 – that 'all knowing' look.

Left to right - Debbie, Katie, Heather, Misty, Hugh, Joan and John. January 2017 photo for the British Showjumping Magazine. Photo with thanks to Dave Cameron photography.

'In his hand is the life of every creature and the breath of all mankind'

Job 12 v 10

CLAIRE SQUIBB
"*He was born to be a star, a true performer with true grit, courage, skill, talent and that all knowing look in his eye*".

ELINE MARTINE (Norway)
"*He was the best mentor one could imagine, he did everything for me. He is one in a million and I loved him very much.*

LENA ULVEN (Norway)
"*We took him to the Sunshine Tour in Spain, everyone came to see the famous British pony. 'Miami' was a superstar down there*".

NORA LARSEN NALBENT (Norway)
"*I was so lucky to have the opportunity to be taught by this amazing teacher of a pony*".

MARK McGOWAN (course designer at HOYS 2006)
"*For a pony like Miami Bound to give the results I hoped for as a course designer on such a big stage is something I will cherish for the rest of my life*".